Selected Writings of
BENJAMIN MORGAN PALMER

Selected Writings of

BENJAMIN MORGAN PALMER

Articles written for
The Southwestern Presbyterian
in the years 1869–70

Selected by Caleb Cangelosi
&
Edited by C. N. Willborn

THE BANNER OF TRUTH TRUST

THE BANNER OF TRUTH TRUST

3 Murrayfield Road, Edinburgh, EH12 6EL, UK
P.O. Box 621, Carlisle, PA 17013, USA

*

First published 2014
© The Banner of Truth Trust 2014
Reprinted 2016

*

ISBN:
Print: 978 1 84871 410 6
EPUB: 978 1 84871 411 3
Kindle: 978 1 84871 412 0

*

Typeset in 11 /14 Adobe Garamond Pro at
The Banner of Truth Trust, Edinburgh

Printed in the USA by
Versa Press Inc.,
East Peoria, IL

Contents

Part Four:
CHRISTIAN PARADOXES

Part Five:
MISCELLANIES ON CHRISTIAN EXPERIENCE

Foreword

THE *Selected Writings of Benjamin Morgan Palmer* will surely appeal to Christian readers across a broad spectrum. As one who has had the honor of being among Dr. Palmer's remote successors, I can say that his life and work have long been a presence in my mind and heart. He was a great theologian; but, far more than that, he was a powerful preacher and a remarkably able pastor. He can have had few peers as an evangelist and a wise physician of souls.

For him no obstacle—no inconvenience, no danger of infectious disease, no distinction of race or class—could keep him from responding to cries for help. When late on a wet and dismal Saturday night, with a Communion Sabbath before him, a summons came and Mrs. Palmer urged him to delay his response until the morning, he replied, 'No. Death waits upon no man's convenience, and an immortal soul may be at stake.' I cannot imagine that any minister of the gospel, or serious Christian, will remain unaffected by Dr. Palmer's wise, patient dealings with stricken souls.

The book gives us far more than that. The articles on Foreign Missions are as relevant now and compelling as when he wrote them a century and a half ago. The same can be said of his exposition of the Beatitudes of Matthew 5 which I think is in a category all its own, as well as what he has to say about 'Christian Paradoxes,' and 'Miscellanies on Christian Experience.'

No expression of mine is adequate to convey the power of this book. It is to be hoped that readers will rise from these incomparable *Selected Writings* to the magisterial *Life and Letters of Benjamin Morgan Palmer*, by Thomas Cary Johnson, also published by the Trust.

JOHN R. DE WITT
Columbia, SC
March 2014

Acknowledgments

A S with any book, there are a number of people to
whom thanks ought to be expressed. Carol, my
wife and friend, was, as always, my number one encour-
ager. Rev. Caleb Cangelosi deserves the bulk of thanks
for doing the difficult work of transcribing these many
articles from very poor quality microfilm. This job was
certainly the most tedious work related to the project.
Caleb also aided with the Introduction by supplying
information about the various materials in this book
and their original publication. Without Caleb's vision
and zeal for this project it would not have been accomplished. Also, thanks is due to Mr. and Mrs. William
Thiessen, faithful members of Covenant Presbyterian
Church, Oak Ridge, Tennessee, for comparing the
transcribed manuscript to the original texts for accuracy. They also made several useful suggestions which
improved the final version.

I am very grateful for Dr. John R. de Witt's careful reading of the text and provision of an excellent
Foreword to this volume. Additionally, I wish to thank

Dr. Richard Phillips, Senior Minister of Second Presbyterian Church, Greenville, South Carolina, for the insightful Afterword and encouragement in this project. Of course, I offer many thanks to Jonathan Watson and the team at the Banner of Truth Trust for taking on this project and bringing it to fruition.

Finally, I want to offer thanks and honor in dedicating this book to our triune God. His eternal Spirit would not let me forget that this good project was worthwhile. May all praise redound to his wonderful name. *Soli Deo Gloria!*

C. N. WILLBORN
Oak Ridge, TN
April 2014

Introduction

B. M. PALMER (1818–1902), wrote Thomas Cary Johnson, 'was sprung of excellent stock, and born into the midst of a civilization at once unique, commanding and noble'. He was born in Charleston of English ancestry to Edward and Sarah Bunce Palmer. His father was a noted pastor in the low country of South Carolina and his uncle, Benjamin Morgan Palmer, was a leading churchman and pastor of the famous Circular Church of Charleston. He carried his uncle's name and possessed the sound convictions and irreproachable reputation of both uncle and father. His station in life was that of a gentleman. He was never disqualified from this station and used it as a platform to proclaim his convictions about man and God, country and cause.

After taking his early education in the low country of South Carolina, he was, like so many Southern young men, sent to the north for college. At fourteen years of age he enrolled at Amherst College. There he studied alongside such men as Stuart Robinson of Kentucky (later to be a Presbyterian educator, author, and pastor) and the older Henry Ward Beecher of Connecticut (of the famous Beecher family) who would champion abolition and, in his later years, be tried for adultery. Beecher and Palmer were favorites of their fellow students, especially notable for their debates. Beecher was known for his florid rhetoric while Palmer's strength was in his 'more classic, more Demosthenian' command of reason. Thomas Cary Johnson informs us that both Beecher and Palmer were drawn to one another not only in debate but 'by a common love for the game of chess'. After a most interesting exit from Amherst, Palmer completed his college studies at the University of Georgia under the classical tutelage of James P. Waddell. Among his classmates at Georgia were future U.S. Supreme Court justices, circuit judges, and John LeConte, MD, LLD, to become President of the University of California.

Palmer pastored several influential urban churches for sixty-two years—First Presbyterian Church, Savannah, Georgia (1841–43), First Presbyterian Church, Columbia, South Carolina (1843–55) and First Presbyterian Church, New Orleans, Louisiana (1856–1902). He also taught in the theological seminary at Columbia, South Carolina on two occasions (1854–56; 1862–63), and gained a national reputation as 'the most magnificent pulpit orator'. In the pulpit or out of it, he was known to be a Presbyterian of Presbyterians as evidenced in his creedal fealty, yet he was also known to possess 'the most inclusive affection for all men'. Upon his death it was said that the crowd that pressed around his open tomb consisted of 'Protestants of every name, Roman

Catholics, priests and people, Jews and men of the world'.

His inclusive affection for all men was evident by his benevolent concern for the black members of New Orleans society, which culminated in the establishment of a black congregation of First Presbyterian Church. But perhaps nowhere is Palmer's generous heart more evident than in the great crises of 1858, '67, and '78 when yellow fever struck New Orleans. He was vigilant in visiting the sick even at what was then considered great risk to himself. He visited every home with the sign of fever in the window, not just those of his own church, and 'got the heart as well as the ear of New Orleans'. Through his self-sacrifice, he became known as 'the pastor to New Orleans'. William McFaddin Alexander, a New Orleans pastor, spoke to this very point:

> Some men are great as statesmen, some as philosophers, some as theologians, some as preachers; but Dr. Palmer was great in whatever relation he sustained. In the pulpit he was without a peer; as a theologian, clear, strong, logical; as a citizen and patriot, second to none. He was a man of convictions. He stood for something, and yet in such a gentle and courteous way that he made thinking men his firm friends, though they occupied positions hopelessly separated from him— witness the remarkable scene in the Jewish Synagogue the other night when Rabbi Leucht prayed for Dr. Palmer's recovery and praised him as a Christian. Yes, they were Jews and they knew he was a Christian, and they honored him as a Christian. That is a gift that few men possess—to be firm and true to one's colors and at

the same time not to be disagreeable and discourteous to those who differ with you.[1]

'Ben Palmer', as he was known in his youth, was not just a brilliant star in the ecclesiastical galaxy, he was, as intimated above, a noted citizen. His public image was notable among South Carolina's educational and political elite, but it grew especially large in New Orleans. His speeches *for* constitutional republicanism and *against* the lottery reveal his willingness to put his great gifts to use for civil good. As a public man, he was always 'ready to help every measure designed to secure justice between man and his fellow man'. For his gallant service, his city and state, as well as his church, recognized and admired 'Dr. Palmer'. This is well illustrated when, in 1890, Col. William Preston introduced him to a large public crowd as 'the first citizen of Louisiana'.

Palmer was not just a talker; he was a doer as well. In April 1862, he left New Orleans to visit Confederate General Albert Sidney Johnston. It is said that he, 'astride a horse, ... delivered a thrilling address to a portion of Johnston's army just before it went into the battle [of Shiloh]'. From this public duty, he was to travel on to Memphis where he would serve in his ecclesiastical capacity at the General Assembly of the Presbyterian Church of the Confederate States of America. Due to the imminent threat to Memphis, however, the General Assembly was moved to Montgomery and Palmer

---

[1] Thomas Cary Johnson, *The Life and Letters of Benjamin Morgan Palmer* (1906; Edinburgh: The Banner of Truth Trust, 1987), pp. 633-634. All unmarked quotes are from this edition.

was pressed into service by Mississippi's governor who wished for him to canvass the State in an effort to rally disaffected citizens (many on the Confederacy's western edge felt little had been done for their protection) around the Cause. He delivered patriotic addresses throughout the state. Of one such address Jackson's *The Mississippian* claimed for Palmer great success, concluding by saying: 'What is said of Lord Brougham may with equal truth be said of Dr. Palmer—"he wields the club of Hercules entwined with roses."'

For his various addresses, and their attending success, Palmer was advised not to return to New Orleans and to remove his family from the city. After all, 'he was looked upon by Union men as an arch rebel and fomenter of treason'. For a brief period he served the army of the West under General Bragg. The duration of the War was lived in his beloved *patria* of South Carolina, where he labored in Columbia Seminary, preached regularly, served the war-beleaguered Presbyterian Church (CSA) in various ways, aided the war effort as public man, and delivered a moving eulogy at the burial of James Henley Thornwell (1812–62).

After the war, Palmer and his family returned to New Orleans where he resumed his ministerial and ecclesiastical labors. A persuasive leader of the Presbyterian Church in the United States (Southern Presbyterian Church), Palmer joined men like John B. Adger, R. L. Dabney, John L. Girardeau and Thomas Peck in maintaining a strong biblical and confessional orthodoxy within the church. It may be argued that some of his particular social views are unacceptable, but then all men have their feet of clay. His positive contributions and ministerial labors, in spite of his weaknesses, made him a respected, and in many ways, model citizen, minister, and churchman. His fruitful life was not one of ease, however, for beside the plagues and war years, he lost five of six children in their youth and his wife, Mary Augusta McConnell, step-daughter of Dr. George Howe of Columbia Seminary, after forty-seven years of marriage. One may read the moving accounts of his family losses in *The Broken Home,* one of Palmer's many publications. Palmer remained pastor of First Presbyterian Church, New Orleans until 1902, when he was struck by a street car, which he thought to be stopping for passengers. After lingering in great pain for twenty days he passed into the presence of his faithful Saviour and God on May 25, 1902. A monument to his name and ministry to the South stands in New Orleans' Metarie Cemetery.

The following pages of pastoral sustenance were first read from March 4, 1869 to April 28, 1870, by subscribers to the *Southwestern Presbyterian.* This weekly newspaper, which ran from 1869 to 1908,[2] was the project

[2] The series ran from vol. 1, no. 1 (25 Feb. 1869) to vol. 40, no. 51 (30 Dec. 1908). In 1909, the *Southwestern Presbyterian* merged with the *Central Presbyterian* and with the *Southern Presbyterian* to form the *Presbyterian of the South.* This paper ran until August 12, 1931, when it merged with the *Presbyterian Standard* and was called *The Presbyterian of the South and the Presbyterian Standard.* In April 1944 the title of this publication was changed to the *Presbyterian Outlook,* which is still published today. Special thanks to Ginny Daley and the staff of the Presbyterian Historical Society (Montreat, NC), and

of Presbyterian churchmen who felt keenly the value of a denominational publication to keep church members abreast of current events and to build them up in the faith. Following the failure of a similar paper out of Mobile, Alabama, the *Southwestern Presbyterian* began to be published in New Orleans, Louisiana. Palmer was associated with the endeavor from its inception, serving as a member of its board and a regular contributor to its pages.[3]

Though several of the articles collected in this book were written anonymously, it is certain that Palmer was the author. R. Q. Mallard, in a letter to Thomas Cary Johnson urging him to write Palmer's biography, lists 'Christian Paradoxes' and 'Leaves from a Pastor's Portfolio' among Palmer's contributions to the *Southwestern Presbyterian*.[4] Johnson assures us that the rest came from the pen of Dr. Palmer as well.[5] He describes Palmer's writing for the newspaper as 'of a devotional, expository,

---

Wayne Sparkman of the PCA Historical Center (St. Louis, MO) for tracking down this 'genealogy' of the *Southwestern Presbyterian*.

[3] Johnson, *Life and Letters*, p. 335. Johnson notes that the Session of First Presbyterian Church in New Orleans, following Palmer's leadership, subscribed for fifty copies of the paper to distribute to the poor of the church (*Life and Letters,* p. 306).

[4] *Ibid.,* p. vii.

[5] *Ibid.,* pp. 336, 340. Palmer later wrote much more in this newspaper, including his reflection concerning reunion with the Northern Presbyterian General Assembly, an expanded version of the 'Christian Paradoxes', and the articles that eventually became the book *The Family, in its Civil and Churchly Aspects*. For more on Palmer's contributions to the *Southwestern Presbyterian*, see Johnson, *Life and Letters,* pp. 335-345. The PCA Historical Center currently has the years 1869-1901 on microfilm.

and practical character',[6] and to that list we might add eloquent, pastoral, evangelistic, polemical, and wise. Palmer's insight into the Word of God and the heart of man is striking; one comes away from these writings thinking that it is little wonder he was able to pastor one church for forty-six years.

These chapters also provide us with a small window into the religious thought and practice of late nineteenth-century Presbyterianism in the American South, of which Palmer was exemplary. One of the things Palmer and a number of his contemporaries model for us is that wonderful Pauline ability to hold to and speak the truth tenaciously, yet in meekness and humility. 'This gift Dr. Palmer possessed as few men have ever possessed it. Hence men of all creeds loved and honored him...'[7]

[6] *Ibid.,* p. 340.
[7] Johnson, *Life and Letters,* pp. 633-634.

PART ONE

---

*Leaves from a
Pastor's Portfolio*

I

Never Too Late[1]

DURING the epidemic of 1867, a pastor in the city of New Orleans was just leaving his study to attend the funeral of one who had fallen a victim to the pestilence. A crumpled note was placed in his hands requesting him to repair immediately to the couch of a dying stranger. Promising to obey the summons as soon as released from the service then present, within an hour he turned sadly away from the cemetery, where the solemn words, 'dust to dust', had just been pronounced, to look again upon Death, struggling with his prey, in a retired chamber.

A single glance revealed the form of an athletic young man, with a broad and noble brow, upon which the seal of the grave was visibly set. Sitting on the edge of the bed, and taking the sufferer's hand kindly in his own, the preacher said, 'Mr. M—, do you know how ill you are?'

[1] Appeared in the *Southwestern Presbyterian*, April 1, 1869.

'Yes', was the quick response; 'I shall soon pass the bourn whence no traveler returns.'

'Are you, then, prepared to die?'

'Alas! No, sir', fell upon the ear like the knell of a lost soul.

'Will you, then, let me pray for you?' And with the assent given, the knee was bowed before him who alone has power to save. In two or three terse sentences, uttered with tremulous emotion, the case of the dying sinner was laid at the mercy seat.

The moments were shortening fast; very soon the last sand would disappear from the hour-glass. The conversation was promptly resumed, as follows:

'Mr. M——, I am told you are the son of pious parents, and have been reared in the bosom of the church; you do not need, therefore, that I should explain to you the way of salvation—for which, indeed, there is now no time. But you know that the Bible says, "God so loved the world that he gave his only begotten Son, that whosoever believeth in him should not perish, but have everlasting life." Only believe *now* in this Savior, and you are saved.'

'Oh! sir', was the reply, 'if God will only spare me this once I promise that I will live very differently in the future than I have lived in the past.'

'My dear friend', rejoined the minister, 'this is the last device of Satan to destroy your soul. I tell you faithfully, there is no future for you in this world; you are now passing, whilst I speak, through the gateway of Death, and what you do, you must do at once, or be lost forever.'

To this appeal the only answer was a deep groan, whilst the beads of moisture, gathering upon that ample forehead, and the swollen veins, drawn like a dark seam across it, betokened the anguish of a guilty spirit, shrinking from the presence of an angry God. A few seconds of awful silence intervened; but a last effort must be made to pluck this soul from the lethargy of despair. 'Mr. M—, do you remember the story of the penitent thief upon the cross? His time was short, just as yours is; but one brief prayer, not longer than a line, expressed his faith, and was enough. So you see that it is never too late.'

At this the closed eyes were opened, and the first word of hope fell from the parted lips: *'No, it is not too late; thank God, it is not too late.'*

'Mr. M—', said the pastor, 'do you trust now in the Lord Jesus Christ?'

'Yes, I do; he is my Savior, and I am not afraid to die!' rung out upon the startled listeners, as though a note from the song of the harpers had fallen from heaven into that chamber of death.

There was another silence of a few seconds—this time a silence of wonder and joy; it was broken by the dying man, as he turned upon his side and whispered to the minister, 'Will you write to my father?'

'Yes, certainly; but what shall I tell him?'

'Tell him I have found Jesus, who has pardoned my sins, and I am not afraid to die; he will meet me in heaven.'

It was his last utterance, for in the next moment the soul, that had passed through this fierce struggle into the second birth, winged its separate flight, and stood before the throne.

The whole interview thus described was shut up within the limits of fifteen minutes, from the moment of entrance into that darkened chamber, till the tenant-less body lay in its cold sweat, to be shrouded for the tomb.

Sad, yet sweet, were the pastor's thoughts as he walked to his home, beneath the stars, through the streets of the silent city: thoughts of the vast solemnity and precious-ness of his office, as an ambassador for Christ: thoughts of that blessed family covenant, by which God remembers the prayers of a believing parent, and looks at the tears in his bottle—sometimes even upon the death-bed of the child: thoughts of that unutterable love which saves, even to the uttermost, and makes it *never too late* to pluck the brand from the burning.

2

Jesus Not a Half Savior [2]

'B—', said my father to me at the breakfast table, the morning after my arrival in one of the visits annually paid to the old homestead; 'do you remember your old schoolmate, H. P.?'

'Perfectly well', was the reply; 'it would take more than twenty years to efface the recollection of the most intimate friend of my childhood.'

'Well', rejoined he, 'he has one foot in the grave, dying of consumption; and he is such an untamed bear that no one can approach him. Possibly you may gain access on the score of old companionship; who knows what, through God's grace, may be the result of your visit!'

Let me here introduce to the reader the person concerning whom the above dialogue was held. H. P. was the only son of a widowed mother, whose indulgent love proved unable to cope with the passions of a headstrong

[2] Appeared in the *Southwestern Presbyterian*, April 8, 1869.

and willful boy. Upon approaching manhood he broke away from every social restraint, and soon lost every trace of virtue. In his swift declension he not only abandoned himself to vice in its lowest associations, but took an insane pleasure in setting public sentiment at defiance, until, for years, he had come to be regarded as an outcast and an outlaw. At the age of thirteen our paths in life diverged, and now, for the first time in twenty years, they crossed again.

Toward noon when the morning hours of exhaustion should be over, the writer turned his steps slowly to the house of his invalid friend, upon the skirts of the village. Memory yielded up its stores from the buried past, at every footfall; the lessons conned together under the master's ferrule; the wild and noisy sports at recess, upon the village green; and the playmates of those halcyon days—some of whom, alas! were sleeping beneath the turf, over whose early graves aged mourners had too sadly wept. And now I was soon to look upon the most melancholy wreck of all! But sombre as these reflections were, they only half prepared me to greet the specter which slowly glided into the parlor, leaning wearily upon a staff, and sinking, exhausted, even at this effort, upon the sofa by my side.

'My dear H., it grieves me to the heart to find you thus.'

'Yes, B—, we have not met for twenty years; and if you had waited a few weeks longer, you must have searched for me in the graveyard of Old Bethel, where the solemn oaks droop with moss over the graves of a century.'

Reader, I had prayed the Lord to make me wise to win a soul, and I was burdened with my prayer. Laying the hand gently upon his knee, I said, affectionately, 'H., do not be angry with me, for the sake of 'auld lang syne', let me tell you what most distresses me; it is that you are half-way into eternity and so unready to die!'

Sepulchral as his own cough was, the melancholy response: 'B——, it is of no use to talk to me on the subject of religion; I am a doomed man—as sure of hell as if already shut up in its vault of fire.'

'Oh! H., my friend, how can you say so?'

'Because, B——, I am a *drunkard!* And no drunkard shall inherit the kingdom of God.' His eye flashed with an unearthly gleam, as he fiercely continued: 'You do not know what sort of a drunkard I am; I carry my jug to bed with me every night—it takes the place of my wife—and I pull from it so often that it can scarcely be said to be corked at all. If I could only break the bonds of this cruel habit, there might be hope for me; but I have tried, a thousand times, in vain; I am bound, hand and foot, with its accursed chains; and there is nothing left to me but to drink and be damned.'

Was it said only to the apostles, 'And it shall be given you in that same hour what ye shall speak'? Instantly I replied to this vehement and self-accusing speech, 'H., you entirely mistake the matter. What you need is a Savior to save you from your drunkenness; he shall be called Jesus, because he shall save his people from their *sins.* The salvation from hell is only the result of this salvation from sin. You must come, dear H., to Jesus, as a drunkard, or not at all.'

With this, we bowed together in prayer, during which the poor emaciated frame shook with sobs, as though it would fall to pieces with the violence by which it was racked.

The interview was too exciting to be longer protracted; and during four days the writer was engrossed with a religious meeting then in progress. At its close, and just before returning to his home, he called to take a final farewell of one whom he was sure never to meet again upon earth. The same pale, wan countenance met his view as before, but now lighted up with a strange and happy radiance.

'B——, a wonderful change has passed over me since you were here, and I do not know what to make of it; it cannot be that I am a converted man?'

'I should not be in the least surprised, H., to find that you are; but tell me all about it.'

'Well', he replied, 'when you went away I prayed God to have mercy upon my poor soul, and all at once the shackles fell off from me, and I have been full of peace and joy ever since.' Pausing for a little fuller statement before committing myself to a reply, he resumed:

'B——, I am a very ignorant man—it is many years since I have been within the walls of a church, and I have forgotten almost everything my pious old mother taught me at her knee. But I want to tell you what I think the gospel is, and where I am wrong you will correct me.' Promising to be very honest in my criticism, he proceeded: 'I think, then, that we are all born into the world with wicked hearts, and are guilty and condemned from our birth; that Jesus Christ has come into the world to save us, if we will only trust entirely in him—but that *he won't be a half Savior to anybody*. I must not do the best I can, and then come to him to complete what remains; but I must come at once, just so, and let him do the whole work, from beginning to end. *He will be a whole Savior, or none.* Is that the gospel?'

Grasping his hand in both of mine, I replied in a voice husky with emotion, 'H., if you had been a Doctor of Divinity for fifty years you could not have put it better'; and, kneeling down on the same spot where we had prayed before, we 'blessed the God and Father of our Lord Jesus Christ, who, according to his abundant mercy, had begotten him again unto such a lively hope'.

Upon reciting the conversation to my venerable parent, I said: 'With your experience and observation, so much larger than my own, would you not take this to be an illustration of Christ's word, "He that hath heard and hath *learned of the Father*, cometh unto me?"'

'Yes', was the reply; 'the natural man receiveth not the things of the Spirit of God, neither can he know them, because they are *spiritually* discerned.'

I returned to my distant home, rejoicing in the conviction that one who had so clearly grasped the central truth of *a whole Savior*, must be born of God. It was, however, a grateful assurance, to learn that after three months of suffering, which yet were brighter with evidences of grace, my poor friend mounted aloft with rejoicing and song into the rest of the redeemed.

3

The Universalist's Death[3]

I N the year 18—, during my early ministry, I learned
from the attending physician, who was a deacon in
my church that a young man in the neighborhood was
extremely ill, and wholly unprepared to die. I repaired
immediately to the sick chamber, where, after a brief
conversation, concerning the nature and extent of the
disease, I introduced the subject of religion, and proposed to pray for the sufferer; with great courtesy, but
with equal firmness, he replied, 'that he would be
truly thankful for my visits as a *friend*, but begged to be
excused from any religious conversation', adding, that
'he was settled on the doctrine of *universal salvation*, and
did not wish his mind disturbed by religious inquiries'.

Compassionating him only the more deeply for this
reply, and hoping to win him by the law of kindness, I
answered that 'if such was his fixed determination my

[3] Appeared in the *Southwestern Presbyterian*, April 15, 1869.

future visits, though greatly trammeled, would be as he desired'.

They were, accordingly, renewed almost daily, accompanied with such delicacies as a sick person might crave, and which an unmarried man, like himself, might not be able to command. Perceiving, however, that he was sinking daily, and knowing death to be inevitable, I frankly said to him one day, as I took his hand and bid him *adieu,* after a longer stay than usual, that 'this was the last visit I should pay him under the conditions he had imposed',—adding, 'that, viewing him as a dying man, soon to stand before his Judge, my conscience would no longer allow me to sink the minister of the gospel into the mere friend of the world; and that while caring for his bodily wants I consented, practically, to eschew the interests of the soul, his blood might be found upon my skirts, and be required at my hands'.

This declaration moved him to tears. Thanking me again and again for the kindness I had shown, he entreated the continuance of my visits, and concluded by saying, 'that although he retained the sentiments he had at first expressed, and desired neither religious conversation nor prayer, he would yield to my wishes rather than forfeit my society', but 'wondered why I could not be satisfied with praying for him at my own house'. I replied 'that I had all along been doing that, with much fervency and sincerity', but repeated 'that the present interview must be the last, unless he allowed me to be, as the Lord had ordained and commanded me, the ambassador for Christ to beseech sinners, like himself, in Christ's stead, to be reconciled to God'.

The case had pressed heavily upon my heart, from the beginning. Of course it was not my design to suppress the testimony for God and his truth; but so long as delay was possible, I hoped by a wise discretion to insinuate myself into his affections, and so to find the acceptable moment for speaking the words of eternal life. But now the end was approaching—the moment had arrived for decision, and I told him, 'that I *dared* no longer refuse to sound the alarm in the ears of one whom I saw sinking rapidly to the grave, and, as I feared, to the regions of woe'. After further conversation upon his critical condition, I told him that I would engage in prayer, to which he raised no further objection, when— in the most solemn and touching manner possible—I commended him to the only Savior who could pluck him from impending ruin; and implored the Spirit's aid and power in renewing his heart, and preparing him for his solemn translation.

Two or three visits were made upon this new footing, in each of which, warnings, admonitions and entreaties were mingled, when, suddenly, the idea seized him that he might be cured under the treatment of an eminent physician in a city not far distant. Preparations were made to convey him to the river; but before leaving I determined to utter what might possibly prove the last warning. Taking his hand, I said, 'My friend, you are very low, and may not live to reach the city, I may never see you again, alive. I have endeavored to be faithful to you, ever since you allowed me to speak freely and tenderly about your soul's salvation; pardon me, if I now frankly, but affectionately, tell you that if you die in your present state of mind, and with your present mistaken views of religious truth, *you are a lost man; your doom is fixed; the heaven, of which you dream, you will never see:* the God of eternal truth has said of the impenitent and unconverted, 'These shall go away into *everlasting punishment!*"' How these words were to break upon him in a thrice terrible reality, I was shortly to witness.

It so happened, through providence, that duty called me to the same city, about the time he expected to arrive. Traveling more swiftly by land, I was at the wharf as the vessel was warped to her mooring. He was lying on the mattress, just where he had been first placed. No sooner had I stepped aboard and his eyes lighted upon me, than he cried out, with passionate vehemence: 'Oh, my friend! kneel down and pray for me. *I am fast going; your warnings are becoming fearfully true: I am a lost man; my doom is sealed.* Oh, pray for me!' Kneeling beside his pallet, I offered up an agonizing prayer for his salvation. Following him to the apartments which had been secured for him, I continued all that day pointing him to the Crucified One, the only and all-sufficient Savior: but the only response was, *'Too late! too late! I am lost: forever lost!'* Leaving him for the night to the attention of his physician and nurse, I returned in the morning to find him near his end. All that was left me *now* was to point him, as a convicted sinner, to the cross, as his only hope, reminding him, among other things, of the dying thief in the gospel, and beseeching him to cast his guilty soul upon the bleeding Lamb. But to all these pleadings, and assurances of God's great mercy, and Christ's rich grace, there was but one reply: *'Too late!—lost!—lost! forever!'* About four in the afternoon he passed away; while the expiring breath bore upon the air the wail of a lost soul: *'I—am going—to',*—death stifled the word which was too awful to hear—it was whispered in eternity!

The foregoing appalling sketch is given almost in the very words in which it was delivered to the writer by a venerable minister, now standing, himself, very near the eternal gates. Across the track of more than forty years, he calls up this frightful specter, which flitted before his vision a moment, and then plunged into the dark abyss.

Reader, it bids you beware how you trifle with *your last* opportunity, lest it become to you a *lost* opportunity. Twice did this wretched young man 'reject the counsel of God against himself', when it was pressed home upon the conscience by the faithful servant of Christ. When, at length, the dark curtain rose before his eyes, displaying the judgment seat and the avenging law, it was too late. The fierce wail went up for help, but was met with the stern rebuke, 'Because I called and ye refused, I stretched out my hand and ye would not regard, but ye set at naught all my counsel, and would none of my reproof; I, also, will laugh at your calamity—I will mock when your fear cometh.' There may be a line, which, like a thread, defines your probation upon earth; a moment when it may be too late to pray—it is 'when God shall swear, saying, "I will not be an healer."'

4

The Young Student[4]

I T was the month of June, and the rays of a golden sun
glanced from the bosom of the broad Mississippi, as
from a burnished mirror. Seated just within the saloon
of the elegant steamer, where the eye was screened from
the dazzling brilliancy without, whilst it feasted upon
the shifting scenery of the distant bank, the writer sur-
rendered himself to those dreamy meditations which so
often hang like a soft mist around the mind of a traveler. His reverie was soon broken by a young man, who
drew up his chair, and modestly opened the following
conversation:

'I trust, sir, that you will not consider me obtrusive in
introducing myself as a student of the University, whose
Commencement Exercises you have just attended, and,
as one of the audience, which listened to your stirring
defense of Christianity.'

[4] Appeared in the *Southwestern Presbyterian*, April 22, 1869.

'On the contrary', I replied; 'I am entirely disengaged, and have a recollection of my own college life fresh enough to secure the warmest interest in every young student I may chance to meet.'

'Well, sir, I find my mind laboring under many difficulties on the subject of religion; and if I can persuade you that I am not actuated by a captious spirit, but by a sincere desire to know the truth, I would like to set them before you, under the conviction that you will be able to resolve them, if anyone can.'

Assuring him that I would listen with the utmost candor, I begged that he would free himself of all restraint, and speak everything that was in his thought.

'I have often desired such an opportunity as this', he replied; 'but have always been afraid to express my doubts to those who could best relieve them, lest I should be written down a Free-thinker, and forfeit the esteem of those whom I revere.'

'In this suspicion you greatly wrong us, my young friend. Ministers of the gospel have wrestled with too many doubts, in reaching their convictions, not to sympathize with the early struggles of others in the search after truth. Doubt', I continued, 'is but the hunger of the mind, the starting point of all inquiry; and you remember, doubtless, that splendid passage of Sir William Hamilton, in which he defines the relation of honest doubt to all knowledge?'

A smile of grateful confidence played upon the ingenuous countenance before me. He had encountered no professional dogmatism, such as he had hinted at in his preliminary protest; and I felt that I had secured a pledge of his candor—so important, if disputation is to be carried to any positive result. This point gained, I invited the statement of his difficulties.

'Oh!' said he, 'the Bible is so full of mysteries, which I cannot comprehend.'

'Granted'; was the reply; 'but what of that?'

'Why, it does not seem reasonable, to me, that I should be required to believe what I do not understand.'

'My young friend', I said; 'will you stick to that?'

This challenge brought up the discussion at a round turn. He paused for a moment, as though measuring the sweep of the admission, and a little suspicious of some discomfiture lying in ambush.

'Why do you hesitate?' I resumed; 'you have stated the principle in broad terms, as universal in its application. If sound in one department of inquiry, it must be equally so in every other; else, it is wholly without value as a critical test.'

'I cannot see', said he at length, 'but that it is a just canon; I will stick to it, wherever it may lead.'

'This skirmishing is not without its use', I added; 'for unless we settle principles at the outset there is nothing to which we can refer as the arbiter between us.' Taking, then, a letter from my pocket: 'Will you write upon the back of this, with your pencil, the fraction, $\frac{1}{3}$, and give me its value in decimals?'

He jotted down upon the blank envelope a string of .333, quite across its length. 'Have you exhausted the fraction?' I asked.

'No', was the reply.

'Well, go on until you do exhaust it.'

'It is of no use; for the exact value will not be expressed though I should extend this line of figures to the North Pole.'

'And yet you tell me that every additional figure brings you one step nearer to that value?'

'Certainly!'

'Well, my friend, if there is one conclusion plainer than another, it is that, if at each step I get nearer to an object, I have only to go on until I reach it.'

'But, my dear sir, that is the doctrine of "the Infinite series", which mathematics demonstrates goes on and never ceases.'

'Precisely so', I replied; 'and I firmly believe it. But what becomes of your fundamental principle of refusing to believe what you cannot comprehend?'

He was evidently stunned by the unexpected retort; drawn, as it was, from the very science which professes to rest upon absolute demonstration, and claims to be certain of its conclusions. 'You are not staggered', I continued, 'at the infinite in mathematics; why should you be scandalized at the infinite in God?'

As my antagonist remained silent, it was not necessary to press the illustration—which some of my readers will perceive to be exactly similar to those employed by Dr. Mason, in his admirable brochure, entitled, *'The Young Traveler'*. 'But', said I, 'let us subject your favorite canon to another test. What is this which I toss in my hand?'

'A gold pencil', was the answer.

'And the point with which it writes?'

'Why, that is lead.'

'Very well. Now tell me, what is gold? and what is lead? and what is it that makes the one to differ from the other?'

He enumerated, with entire accuracy, the different properties of the two metals, and then paused. 'So far, so good', I rejoined; 'you have described the special qualities of the two, by which they may be distinguished. You have told me, in other words, a good deal *about* them both—perhaps all that can be known, but you have not yet stated what either exactly is. You are too much of a scholar to confound the *accidents* with the *essence*. I wish to learn what that is in both these metals, which underlies their respective properties, and which makes the one not to be the other; you call it *substance;* but what is substance, but the unknown and incomprehensible *something* in which outward and inscrutable qualities inhere, and which renders what we behold a true entity?'

'All our knowledge of matter', he replied, 'is relation; that is to say, we know its properties, and the laws or conditions under which they are manifested. But the essence of things transcends our knowledge, and must be assumed as a final fact, attested by the existence of the qualities which must belong to some substance, as the ground of their being.'

'All that I can readily receive; but how you can do it, my young friend, in the face of your original principle, which rejects the incomprehensible as an object of faith, I can scarcely reconcile with logical consistency.'

'I am perfectly satisfied', the student frankly replied; 'and I thank you for rending the skepticism in which I was entangled.'

'And yet, do you perceive that I have not solved any one of your many difficulties?'

'You have done more, sir; in showing the falsity of the principle upon which they all rested, I see clearly that the same difficulties meet me in the sphere of the natural as of the supernatural; and that I must either discard my infallible test, or plunge into universal doubt and unbelief.'

'Precisely the point to which I desired to lead you', I replied. 'The fact is, the supernatural touches you everywhere; you cannot move a dozen paces in any path of science before you bring up against the unknown; and all the inductive sciences really found at last, upon faith. Facts, not yet understood, are accepted simply as facts, each upon its own testimony. We, then, classify and compare, ascending from the lower generalization to the higher, until we eliminate the grand formula, or law, under which they are produced. Lay down, however, the canon, at the outset, that we may not believe what we do not comprehend, and the very basis is destroyed upon which your whole induction rests.'

'That is transparently true in physical science', he rejoined.

'Much more then must the principle be false in religion', I added, 'where the subjects presented to our view are, in their very nature, transcendental. Whoever undertakes to carry it out, consistently, will find himself master of a very short creed. The doctrine of the Trinity is discarded because we cannot understand how God can be both one and three—as though these two propositions were affirmed of the Divine Being in precisely the same sense. Thus the mystery of the incarnation is abandoned because we cannot comprehend how the two poles of being shall be united in the same person, without mixture or confusion. But not to insist upon these higher mysteries, whoever conceived, rightly, of God's absolute eternity—without successions of time, but an eternal and present NOW? Who can explain how God *knows?* which is not by passing from mere premises to conclusions, as with us, but by one infinite, all-embracing thought; so that, by one movement of the magician's wand, God and nature both disappear, and leave you and me in a universe that is blank. The principle, therefore, with which you started, must be discarded, or you are left a prey to absolute pyrrhonism.'

'I see it! I see it!' responded my young friend; 'and I shall turn, now, with more docility to the teachings of Scripture, where God has been pleased to record his testimony of the supernatural.'

'And may God give you the true wisdom, that you may know him who is the eternal life', was the benediction under which this interesting dialogue was closed.

5

The Reformed Inebriate[5]

I WAS seated one Friday evening in my parlor, enjoying the society of a few friends by the family fireplace, when the door-bell rang, with a hesitating sound, as if touched by a weak or a trembling hand. Obeying the summons, myself, without waiting for a servant, the dim light of the street revealed a stranger, who addressed me thus:

'I presume you are the Rev. —, if so I would be glad to speak to you alone, in your study.'

Ushering him upstairs into the little back room, where, each week, the olive oil is beaten for the lamps of the sanctuary, the lighted gas disclosed a form in which it was impossible not to be immediately interested. He was a little above the average height, with a well-knit frame and a graceful carriage, which betrayed him as familiar with good society. A broad forehead—which seemed

[5] Appeared in the *Southwestern Presbyterian*, April 29, 1869.

the more expansive as it merged into a perfectly bald crown—and the clearly cut and compressed lips, were symbols alike of character and intellect. The eye, alas! which should have expressed even more, was blood-shot and streaked with veins, while the entire countenance was haggard and flushed. I had scarcely time for a super-ficial glance, when he sank upon a chair, and bowed his head between his arms, crossed upon the table, and in that position he sobbed aloud for the space of ten min-utes. Satisfied that I was in the presence of a gentleman who would soon be able to assert himself, and direct the interview, I waited patiently for this paroxysm of feeling to pass by, without interposing a word.

Lifting himself, at length, he turned his face upon mine, and in choice language recited his personal his-tory, substantially as follows:

'You have before you, sir, a man who has fallen from the highest social position to the lowest degradation. At an early age I was left to the care of a widowed mother, and was reared with all that fond affection likely to be lavished upon an only child. I was furnished with the advantages of a liberal education, and entered, at my majority, upon the possession of a handsome estate. Pros-ecuting the study of the law, and admitted to its practice, I was rising gradually in that profession, which promised to reward me with honorable distinction. In due course of time I was united in marriage with a lovely wife, whose intellectual gifts, personal charms, and amiable temper, are such as seldom have blessed a human home. And, to crown the whole, I was a professor of religion, and esteemed a worthy member of the church of God. In the midst of all this earthly prosperity, whilst life was blooming around me like the ancient paradise, I was seized, two years ago, with the insane desire of becoming suddenly rich, and yielded to the temptation of abandoning my profession, in order to speculate in whisky! Separated by my new calling from the sweet influences of home, and surrounded by the associations which belong to such a traffic, I have fallen a victim to its baneful power, and am now before you a degraded sot! upon the verge of *delirium tremens*. The two weeks that I have spent in your city have been spent in a deep debauch. These two letters (which he took from a side pocket) have been lying, unanswered, all that time; and not till this afternoon have I been sober enough to break the seals, and learn their contents. I have, however, read them over and over again, and you see they are blotted and stained with my tears. I am overwhelmed with remorse; listen to them, and see how they plead with such a wretch as I am!'

Choking with the emotion which often interrupted the perusal, he then unsealed and read to me the first of these letters; it was from his mother, and a more eloquent and pathetic appeal never flowed, even from a mother's pen. It began with her early widowhood, when 'the strong staff was broken, and the beautiful rod' upon which she had leaned. It told how her bruised affections had gathered around the only child spared to be the comfort of those weary years; and her heart had grown warm with hope as this boy developed into manhood. It described the fullness of her gratitude when these hopes seemed to be realized in the rich promise of his later years, and the proud joy she felt when, in his pride, she clasped a daughter in her arms. It depicted the beauty of his home, where, now, two prattling babes whispered the name of the absent father. Then came the fearful contrast: how the tempter entered into this Eden, and with him the blighting of hopes, and the ruin of her son. Upon the back of all this, poured the passionate entreaty—breaking, like a wail, from a dying woman's heart—that the wanderer would come back to the endearments of home, and walk, evermore, in the paths of honor and virtue. The appeal was enough to move a heart of stone. It made me, a stranger, weep; no wonder that he, to whom it was addressed, shook beneath its breath, like a reed before the storm.

He then opened the second letter. It began: *'My Darling Husband.'* Ah! this tenderness of a still loving wife; it cut with an edge keener than that of reproach—to the very core of his remorse. Throwing the sheet upon the table, he covered his face with his hands, and sobbed—without an effort at self-control. It was too much for me, as well as for him, so I put out my hand, gently, to his, and said, 'Put up that letter, Mr. B., it is from your wife; and let no one come into the sanctuary of that confidence. I was not unwilling to hear the pleadings of your mother—the words of a wife are too sacred.'

Replacing the letters in his pocket, he turned and said with something like vehemence, 'My dear sir, will you pray for me?' Kneeling down together, I poured forth one of those wrestling prayers in which the argument grows, and the fervor deepens, as we advance, that it would please God to change this remorse into penitence; that the blood of Christ might purge this conscience, groaning under a sense of guilt; that the Holy Spirit might renew and save this poor sinner, upon whom God had so just and perfect a claim. Scarcely had we risen before he cried out, 'Oh! sir, pray for me again!' We knelt a second time; and so a third—and then a fourth—a fifth; when the sixth request came I paused, and said, 'Mr. B——, this scene is becoming oppressive; I am afraid that we are in danger of those vain repetitions which the Savior condemns. It is right that we should go to God in prayer, for he is the only source of grace and strength to you in this hard battle with your vices. But we have told it all to God, and now he waits to hear from your own lips what you mean to do.'

'Do!' said he; 'what *can* I do?'

'My friend', I replied; 'something else is required of you besides prayer; and by the very solemnity of the petitions we have offered here together, I summon you to decide what course you intend to pursue in the future.'

'Tell me, sir, what I ought to do.'

'Well, then, in the first place, you must extricate yourself from the accursed business which has been your ruin. Were I you, I would take the hogsheads of liquor you came here to sell, to the levee, and empty them all into the waters of the Mississippi.'

'Ah, sir, I cannot do that, for I have partners equally implicated in the speculation.'

'Then, at any rate, wash your hands of the whole business at once; will you do this?'

'Yes, sir, I will, if I live to see tomorrow's sun.'

'In the next place', I resumed; 'go back, at once, to your neglected home, and there, under the sanctity of your widowed mother's prayer, and beneath the softening influences of your wife and babes, foster the purpose of reform. Resume the practice of your noble profession; and throw around yourself all the restraints and obligations of society. Will you do this?'

'I will, sir', was the instantaneous response.

'Once more: I am bound in faithfulness to say to you that I have little confidence in the unaided strength of the human will to break the fetters of such a vice as holds you in its grasp; and none at all in the sinner's ability, without divine grace, to repent, truly, before God. Go, then, in your guilt and helplessness, to him whose promise is, "though your sins be as scarlet, they shall be as white as snow", and throw yourself upon his mercy, in Christ, for pardon and eternal life.'

'I can only promise, my dear sir', was the response, 'to make an honest effort to obey your counsel in respect to this.'

'What I wish to impress upon you, my friend', I replied, 'is, that remorse is not repentance, and reformation is not religion. Renew the covenant which you have broken, with your God; and do not rest until you have a sense of your "acceptance in the beloved".'

Upon parting with him at the door, I said, 'Mr. B—, do not touch a drop tomorrow, and come the next day to hear me preach.'

On the following Sabbath I looked anxiously around the church for my visitor, in whose welfare I was now deeply interested; and, sure enough, over the gallery, not far from the pulpit, peered the face and head which could not be mistaken. I had found no difficulty in the selection of my theme, for the only dark feature of the conversation above narrated, was the disposition to throw the blame of his fall upon circumstances which had shaped his course. This danger I now sought to disclose, by choosing that passage from James which read: 'Let no man say, when he is tempted, I am tempted of God; but every man is tempted when he is drawn away of his own lust', *etc*. Tracing the genealogy of sin, as here taught, I attempted to show that outward temptations derive their power from the inclinations and state of our own hearts, as congenial therewith; that in every case of transgression, the sinner must assume the blame of his own misconduct; and that any attempt, however disguised, to throw it back upon God, involved the highest absurdity and self-contradiction, and added, immensely, to the guilt. The following day he called at my door to bid me *adieu,* as he proposed that evening to return to his home in the west, and said, 'You preached that sermon for me, on yesterday.'

'Yes', I answered, 'for once in my life I was intensely personal in the pulpit; I had no one in my thoughts but you; I meant every word to be appreciated by you.'

'I thank you for it', was the response; 'it was exactly what I needed. I see clearly, now, that I have been the author of my own ruin, and have no one to blame but myself.'

'Unless you distinctly recognize your own guilt', I answered, 'you will never deal honestly with God in your repentance. Take the whole burden to him, with perfect assurance that he will never turn the true penitent away, who pleads for mercy in the name of Christ, the Redeemer.'

Some years elapsed—four of them years of bitter sectional war—'ere I had tidings of the poor returning prodigal. But shortly after my own restoration, from a long exile, to my own charge, a newspaper came to me, which, on being unfolded, contained a beautiful address, delivered at a Sabbath school anniversary, in the State of —. The next mail brought me a letter from my lost friend, stating that he had gone back to his home; regained the practice of his legal profession; had sought pardon, and had found peace through the blood of Christ, and was then serving as the superintendent of the Sabbath School, and as a ruling elder in the house of God. Unfortunately, before this letter could be answered, as my grateful heart prompted, it was mislaid, and the address forever lost. If, by any chance, this sketch should meet his eye, the writer prays that it may be accepted as an invitation to reopen the intercourse so abruptly closed.

6

'I Have Done Giving Him Up'[6]

SUCH was the exclamation of a young widow, the joy of whose life had just been crushed out by the remorseless hand of death. Let me introduce her to the reader's pity, by sketching the outline of her great loss:

In the writer's early pastoral charge, there grew up a youth of exuberant promise. His finely chiseled and expressive features reflected the workings of a noble intellect; while an easy and graceful carriage betrayed the child of fortune, who had been reared under the balmiest social influences. Superior natural talents had been generously cultivated in the best schools of science—both at home and abroad—which were still further enlarged by the observation afforded in foreign travel. Without a vice to throw its stain upon a hundred virtues, he grew up in all the symmetry of a perfect manhood, and entered upon the practice of the healing art, with the brilliant prospect of ultimate distinction.

[6] Appeared in the *Southwestern Presbyterian,* May 13, 1869.

The bride, whom ere long he led to the altar, was not beautiful, in the ordinary sense of that abused word; but a sprightly simplicity of character, united with a rare enthusiasm, threw around her a charm, almost indescribable. It was a perpetual dew, resting upon the fresh, moist flower. Hers was not that brusque candor, which is often nothing more than the sting of the wasp—assumed, only for the privilege of spurting out captious and cutting criticisms, and always the most offensive manifestations of egotism. She had that gentle and loving nature, which was transparent, just because it was guileless. Her pure thoughts and sweet affections came bubbling up from the heart to the lips, like the waters in a limpid spring, by the simple necessity of being rendered. At unexpected turns, some bright, fresh word would thrill you, by its sudden revelations of a true, earnest soul, which could afford thus to think itself aloud. It was wonderful, this combination of childhood's artless innocence, with the ripe maturity of the woman—those rich deep utterances of the educated heart, trickling forth in the accents of youth's primitive purity. And it was a rare providence which mated these dissimilar natures in the marriage bond: the eagle, with the strong wing to beat the air, and the clear eye to look upon the sun—and this little songstress, springing out of the morning dew, and caroling her notes of joy, simply because she could not help warbling them upon the air.

Without offspring, these two grew into each other with the advancing years; he, gathering this crystal heart in the folds of his manly and proud love;—and she, wrapping the fibers of her very life around 'the strong staff' and 'the beautiful rod', given for her support. Alas! the strong staff and the beautiful rod were soon to be broken! The years of 1853 and 1854 will not be forgotten, at least by those whose most precious memories lie beneath the shadow of their gloom. The angel of pestilence flapped his black wings over one of our southern cities, in whose silent streets the living walked only in melancholy processions, behind the dead. It was a bright day, in August, when the sun glared with such an eye of mockery upon the suffering earth, that our young physician, exhausted with watching and toil, lay down to rest. Fifteen years have passed since then, and he rests still.

Let us not, too rudely, lift the veil from the young widow's heart. There is no pain like the killing of a nerve—and she possessed that fearful gift of susceptibility which thrills, either with the raptures of joy, or with the tortures of woe. The wild piercing shriek subsides at length into the low and plaintive wail with which the moaning heart eases itself of its pain; and in the darkened chamber, a loving attendance watches the slender form, draped in black, and wilting under its anguish. Here let us, for months, leave the poor mourner alone, with her memory and her God. Alone! to struggle with her great agony, and to conquer it.

Another spring bathes the earth in its soft light, and clothes it with the beauties of a resurrection. It is the middle of the forenoon, and a pale face lifts itself, between the weary stitches, to look upon a daguerreotype,[7]

[7] An early form of photograph.

lying open, on the work basket before her. Tread softly, mother, as you come from the cares of the household, into this quiet sanctuary. Tread softly, and speak gently, lest you bruise a heart, the bitterness of whose woe even you have not yet tasted.

'Oh! Mary, why will you thus feed a grief, whose slow fires are consuming your life away?'

'Mother, you are mistaken: I am not grieving, but only loving. God has taken him, and *I have done giving him up.*'

Reader, there is nothing else to tell; and if there was, I would have you pause here upon this word, which embodies a whole volume of Christian doctrine, and embalms the experience of a life. The end of all discipline is to bring the creature's will into perfect subjection to that of the Creator. It is written of our blessed Master himself, 'Though he were a son, yet learned he obedience by the things that he suffered.' Suffering is not appointed for the sake of suffering, but as the path to a ready obedience. The necessity for this arises from the fact that man's apostasy consisted in setting up the human will in opposition to the divine; which grace, if it be remedial at all, must exactly reverse, enthroning Jehovah, evermore, upon his supremacy. But, alas! how often is there a striving after submission, which is yet not actually reached? How few can say, with the subject of this brief sketch, that it is a thing *done!* We speak of a *submission*, not *merging*, of our will into that of God, after the modern mystics—who seek to engraft the ancient stoicism upon the gospel of Christ. Submission is rather the personal homage which, in the full consciousness of our own individuality, we render to the will of a supreme and loving Father. And until it is reached as the final and habitual posture of our hearts, there remains the necessity for continued discipline, until 'every thought is brought into captivity to the obedience of Christ'. Happiest they who can earliest say:

Thy will, my God, Thy will be done,
And let that will be mine.

7

The Skeptic's Confession[8]

EARLY in the month of January, 1838, I was returning, after the long vacation, to resume my studies
in the University of Georgia, which, some months later,
sent me, with its academic blessing, adrift into the world.
The sabbath had placed its arrest upon me in the city of
Augusta; a cold, rainy, disagreeable day, through whose
weary hours I shivered in one of those bare, thin, fireless
rooms, into which the long corridor of the hotel was
sliced. The longest day will end at last, and night had
thrown its dark mantle over the earth, as I stood before
the huge fire in the common reception room, cheating
the bed, whose scant comfort I had already sufficiently
tested, of at least one hour of tossing and weariness.
Almost touching me, was a tall gentleman, seated in
the corner, and toasting his feet before the ruddy blaze
upon the ample hearth; who, under the pressure of the

[8] Appeared in the *Southwestern Presbyterian*, May 20, 1869.

social instinct, addressed to me a common-place about the uncomfortableness of the day.

'Uncomfortable enough', I replied; 'especially to one locked up, like myself, in a gloomy cell, which only lacks the iron grating to be the fit abode of a criminal, the only relief from which was the brief hour spent at church, in the worship of God.'

This reference to the sanctuary brought a singular smile over the face of the stranger—it was one of those cold smiles, without a gleam of sunshine, and in which rested rather the dark shadow of a sneer. But he was too polite to retain the expression longer than an instant—it had vanished almost before it was detected. Then followed other questions and answers—all common-place enough, as to the preacher's name, the characteristics of the discourse, and the impressions of ability which it had produced. Evidently it was only the social strategy of the skirmisher, beating around to find some topic of common interest upon which conversation might be enjoyed; yet, insipid as the dialogue was, the strangeness of the theme in such a place had already caught the ear of the bystanders; and before either of us was aware there was a profound stillness in the room, which suddenly drew the attention of both to the incongruity of the scene.

Rising, presently, from his seat, the stranger passed to and fro the long hall without, until, catching my eye, he beckoned to me with the finger, and said, 'This is no place for either of us, but come up with me to my room, where I have a fire, for I suspect the hours drag heavily with both of us.'

It was a carpeted and well-furnished chamber into which I was introduced, over whose walls a bright coal fire threw its cheerful glow. Adjusting his slippers to his feet, and sitting down in an easy chair, my friend—as I must now term him, turned to me and said:

'I infer from your manner, as much as from what you said, below stairs, that you are a professor of religion; and I would like you to state upon what grounds you rest your belief that the Bible is a revelation from God.'

I mentioned the external evidences, especially as derived from miracle and prophecy. The first, however, he entirely disallowed, upon Hume's principle, that the evidence being far more abundant for the permanency of nature than for the irregularity of the miracle, this could never be sufficiently authenticated to our belief.

The reader will remember that I was a youth, and an undergraduate, wholly unfamiliar with a discussion which was only brought to my notice by the studies of later years. He will not, therefore, wonder at the embarrassment which this plausible assault upon the miracles occasioned at the time. I ventured, however, to reply:

'The form of your objection seems to me to concede the *value* of the miracle, provided the reality of it could be established; for you admit it to be such an irregularity from the course of nature, as can only be effected through divine power. I hold you, then, to this admission, if the miracle should happen to be proved.'

'Yes', was the response; 'the issue which I make is that no amount of testimony for the miracle can equal the testimony against it, hence it can never be accredited to us.'

'But', I rejoined, 'the *negative* testimony of a thousand witnesses that they have never seen a miracle, cannot set aside the *positive* testimony of three witnesses who have seen it. Both testimonies may be true—and the one does not cancel the other, simply because they are not necessarily contradictory. The difficulty you have to explain is to account for this positive testimony, which upon your supposition, seems to be an effort, without a producing cause.'

'It is far more reasonable', he replied, 'to suppose these few persons to be mistaken, through some deception of the senses, than to set aside the universal experience of mankind as to the uniform operation of natural laws.'

'With all deference to your superior knowledge', I answered, 'this appears to me a simple assumption, and begs the question at issue. We have a chain of historical evidence that certain alleged miracles were wrought, as, for instance, the resurrection of Lazarus, in the presence of Mary, who had every disposition to sift the facts to the bottom—and who never denied them when they occurred—and these facts, admitted to record when they were yet recent, have been handed down to us upon the report of history. If the delusion was not exposed at the time by those who were openly pledged to the detection, I submit that it is too late to raise the question as to the reality of the facts.'

'Very adroitly put', said my friend; 'but you mentioned prophecy, also.'

'Yes', I answered; 'and what do you say to this branch of evidence?'

'Simply that the predictions being assigned to those distant and almost prehistoric ages, one can scarcely help suspecting them to have been manufactured and fitted by ingenious priest-craft to the corresponding events.'

'Pardon me', I replied, 'for saying that this is exactly what you are bound to demonstrate. You forget, too, that it is incumbent upon you to explain the priest-craft itself. It will not do to say that the earth rests upon the horns of a bull, and the bull stands upon the back of a tortoise, while the tortoise rests upon nothing.'

'How then would you state the argument from prophecy?'

'Why, that many clear predictions, as, for example, those respecting the birth and death of Christ, were published and known several centuries before the events occurred in which they are alleged to have been fulfilled. If you do not accept the argument, then you are forced to show, historically, that those utterances were not made prior to the corresponding events, or else that these latter do not furnish a satisfactory fulfillment of them. Besides, there are clusters of predictions remaining yet to be accomplished, by which God proposes to freshen the stream of evidence, to the end of time. Your skepticism is, therefore, in danger of overthrow, at any moment, by the fulfillment of what you cannot deny has been matter of record for at least two thousand years.'

'But', rejoined my friend, 'you do not pretend, at your age, to have gone through the scientific investigation of all these points—much less that the thousands of unlettered Christians rest their faith upon considerations of this sort?'

'No', I replied; 'these external evidences are indispensable in the theoretical defense of Christianity. But the practical faith of man rests, I suppose, upon the internal proof which the Bible furnishes within itself, for—like the sun—it proves itself by its own light.'

'Ah!' said he, 'the Bible is just what you make it, through your interpretations. What seems, in your exposition, a system of glorious and supernatural truth, appears to another a mass of confusion and contradiction.'

'Every man', I responded, 'is responsible for the views he entertains of a great system like that of the Bible. The petulance with which others may dismiss it, in the waywardness or indolence of unbelief, does not cancel this personal obligation to examine it with attention and candor. Postulating a few data, drawn from the assurances of our individual consciousness, the Bible builds up a system unique in its character, and gigantic in its proportions; yet covering truths so transcendental, that they could never be deduced from reason.'

'Particularize, if you please, in a few instances, what you mean.'

'Well, there is the question which has been ringing over the ages, and which philosophy has never been able to solve: "What is the chief good?" The Bible answers it by proposing God, himself, in his infinite perfections, as the everlasting portion of the soul. There is, again, the incarnation, by which the chasm is bridged between the infinite and finite; and which—though shadowed forth in the ancient mythology—you do not, substantively, find, until you meet with it in Christianity. Again, there is redemption and atonement, by which the sinner's salvation is achieved upon eternal principles of law, and to which the natural sense of justice in the human breast is obliged to respond. Further, still, there is the resurrection of the body, which, with all its surrounding symptoms, the reason accepts as the consummation of the soul's immortality—and in their ignorance of which the ancients were unable to complete their doctrine of a future state. And, lastly, there is the new birth, by which the soul is cleansed from the defilement of sin, and fitted for communion with God—of which renovation no other religious system, but that of the Bible, breathes the first hint. In short', I added, 'the argument is wonderfully cumulative. These illustrations may be indefinitely multiplied; but all, like the radii of a circle, conduct to one central conclusion—that the Bible is from God.'

'That', said my friend, 'is the ring bolt from which the whole chain is suspended. How do you fasten the two together?'

'Each one of these thoughts', was the response, 'is a separate intellectual fact, for the existence of which we are obliged to account. If they all lie beyond the orbit of reason, they must have been let down into the human mind by a revelation from God; otherwise, you have an effect without a cause.'

The conversation above recited was, of course, more discursive than is given in this summary, for it was protracted beyond the hour of midnight. Rising, at length, to take my leave, my unknown friend took my hand in both of his, and addressed me in these impressive words:

'My young friend, your faith is better than my skepticism; and if it were simply a matter of will, I would gladly exchange my doubts for your credulity. If I have stated these, it was not with the view of shaking your belief, but because they are extorted by my own wretchedness. You see one before you who is satiated with life; who has wealth enough to gratify even a luxurious taste; who has achieved some of the higher distinctions at the bar; with a bright home, the joy of which is only dashed by the loss of a cherished wife. Yet, in the midst of an enviable prosperity, I am weary of existence, and without positive convictions on the subjects of greatest interest to the human heart. I know not how I have poured these confidences into the ears of a stranger, and of a stripling. In concession to my weakness, make no effort to identify me. Let us part, as we have met— nameless and unknown; and may the God of your faith prosper and make you a happier man than myself!'

I could not listen to such an address unmoved, and replied: 'Forgive my presumption, my dear sir, in saying that yours is not the first noble spirit that has outgrown the earth, and yet refuses to assert its high privilege of communion with the Holy and the True. Do not let Christianity be prejudiced in your esteem by the weak defense of a boy who knows little beyond the traditions of his childhood; but go to him who is the Essential Truth, and kindle your torch at the original source of light and life.'

Thus, like two barks that meet and speak each other on the trackless ocean, we parted. Thirty years have rolled away! Perhaps, he has long since been gathered to his fathers; but if we should meet to-morrow, neither has the clue to the other's identity. But we shall meet at the judgment bar, to face, together, the results of that remarkable interview.

8

A Morbid Experience[9]

SOON after my settlement at —, I was called to see a lady in deep affliction, from the recent death of a father, to whom she was tenderly attached. The flood-gates of feeling now opened at the first touch of Christian sympathy; but there was a manifest reserve during a prolonged conversation, which I attributed to the fact that it was her first interview with a stranger. But, as the pastor so often finds, no sooner had we bowed together in prayer, than all this embarrassment melted away, like the mist of the morning. A new relation had sprung up in that act of common devotion, discovering itself as soon as we had risen from our knees, in hint after hint, until it fairly leaked out that a deeper cause for sorrow existed than even the sore bereavement which had drawn from me so many expressions of condolence. She was in a state of profound darkness as to any sense of her personal interest in the Redeemer. Eleven years

[9] Appeared in the *Southwestern Presbyterian,* May 27, 1869.

before, in obedience to the dictates of conscience, and the instruction of her religious guides, she had united with the church of God, but had never enjoyed one ray of Christian comfort during that long period.

It was a startling revelation! And for the moment I was perplexed how to deal with an experience so entirely new to me. Plainly, the probe must be used, but with great caution and tenderness, for the heart before me was palpitating with grief, and in a condition the least favorable to analyze its own emotions.

'Has it ever occurred to you', I ventured gently to suggest, 'to throw away a hope which brings you so little peace, and to view yourself as a stranger from God?'

A visible shiver passed over her frame, under this touch of the probe.

'A thousand times', she replied; 'but just as often I have felt that I should die, outright, if ever I let go my hold upon the Savior.'

'You have, then, all these years, been trusting in Christ, in the dark, without one smile of his love to cheer you?' I asked.

'Yes', was the response; 'there has never been a moment in all these gloomy years when I could bear to part with even this feeble, comfortless hope; it is all that has kept me from despair.'

It was impossible to listen to the trembling pathos in her tones, without the conviction that here was 'a bruised reed', which must not be broken; 'the smoking flax', which must not be quenched. A cold recital cannot convey to the reader the living impression produced in her presence, that hers was an instance of the most naked faith I had ever witnessed. Here was a soul, cleaving to Christ through years of spiritual darkness, with absolutely nothing between itself and despair but its own faith—a faith, too, unsupported by any of the joys which should prove its stimulus and nourishment.

But the problem was, how a true faith could be exercised through so many years, without the peace which is usually its certain accompaniment. At first a solution seemed to be afforded in the physical prostration of one who was a permanent invalid. Through her adult life she had been subject to frequent and distressing spasms, during the continuance of which she would lie rigid and speechless upon her bed; and then, for days, would be unable to endure the gentlest whisper, or the softest tread, in her darkened chamber. Might not a chronic and constitutional disorder, like this, throw a constant depression upon the spirit, fatal to its elasticity, and preventing it from rising into the region of hopefulness and joy? The suggestion, however, was not satisfactory to her, or to myself. This might account for an experience generally sombre; but it still remained inexplicable that, in the intermissions of rest, there should be no occasional flashes, at least, of pious enjoyment. It seemed that some spiritual cause must exist for a spiritual history so peculiar. At length I said to her, 'Madam, of course you pray?'

'Yes', said she, 'habitually; but without one ray of comfort.'

'Do you pray, then, simply from a sense of duty?'

'Not exactly', she replied; 'I feel constantly like one who is sinking in deep water, and I am obliged to cry out to God for help.'

'Have you no evidence, at any time', I asked, 'that your prayers are answered?'

'Only in this, that I do not wholly despair. I suppose I must be helped; but I have no feeling of communion with God.'

'Well, my dear madam, be so good as to detail to me the general feelings with which you engage in prayer, and what appears to you to be a hindrance to that communion.'

'I scarcely kneel down', she replied, 'before the question obtrudes itself—what right has such a sinner as you to pray? By whichsoever of his titles I address God, the thought seems that the use of such a name is, upon my lips, a mockery. With every petition comes the harrowing suggestion that my claim to any promise is sheer hypocrisy. I try and try, but in vain, to escape from this frightful bondage.'

Here, then, was the secret discovered, at last; this morbid introspection, so persistently indulged, that it had become chronic—the soul turning in upon itself for comfort, and scrutinizing its own exercises, until they had wound up into an inextricable tangle. The key to the mystery was found; but now the trouble was to suggest a remedy. A simple exposition of the difficulty would go but a little way towards its removal; and I saw, clearly, that it would prove almost a life-struggle to break up an incorrigible habit. I rose to leave, that I might gain time for reflection, when she addressed me with much feeling, nearly as follows:

'I have never before breathed a whisper of this to any human ear. I have walked in darkness, and only God has known it. You have drawn it out with a gentle solicitation, to which I have insensibly yielded. You have come to be my pastor, and I am glad that the confession is now made. But will you leave me without saying a word for my relief?'

I replied: 'My dear madam, I think I have the clue to your difficulty; but I want to reflect a little upon what you have stated in this conversation, and in a few days I will be better prepared to give you practical advice.'

Reflection, however, only confirmed the impressions already made, and satisfied me that I had formed what a physician would term a true diagnosis. After the interval of a week I returned to the house of my friend, and said:

'Mrs. G—, the counsel I am about to give will appear to you so heretical that your first impulse will be to reject it at once. But if you have any confidence in me as a religious adviser, I ask that you will defer to my judgment so far as to try, fairly, the experiment which I shall propose.'

'I confide fully in your wisdom', she replied, 'and will follow your counsel to the letter.'

'Well, madam, you are about leaving for the north, to be gone for five months. Understand, then, that I forbid all self-examination until you return. You are not to ask yourself one single question, whether this or that feeling is right or wrong, while you are away. Abandon all reading which describes the experiences of others. Select, on the contrary, those books which hold up Christ in the beauty of his person, and in the glory of his work; and force yourself to meditate upon his essential excellence, rather than to review your own emotions in regard to him. And when you return, in the autumn, we will talk further of these matters.'

'You surprise me beyond measure', was her reply. 'Is not self-examination distinctly enjoined in the sacred Scriptures as one of the most important and sacred of all our duties?'

'True enough', I replied; 'but you have been doing nothing else these eleven years, and it is necessary now to break up this habit from its foundations, that you may begin your religious history over again. You have been burrowing, like a mole, in your own experience, until, like a mole, you have scarcely any eyes with which to see Christ. Let us reverse this order, entirely, for five months, and we will see how the experiment works.'

'I have given my promise', she rejoined, 'and will throw myself blindly upon your guidance.'

And so we parted.

The frosts of early winter had embrowned the leaves of the forest before I was permitted to extend my hand in affectionate greeting of my patient. But there was a beautiful sparkle in her eyes, as she said, 'I owe you a boundless gratitude for untying the knot of my past experience. At first it was almost infinitely hard to follow your counsel; it positively blocked every thought, and brought me up every moment against a dead wall. I feared that I should be forced to abandon the effort as hopeless; but then I saw that my whole life had been a sad mistake; that I had been doing nothing else but walk around "the chambers of imagery", in my own heart. Nothing short of the effort to break up the habit, altogether, could have given me so clear a sense of its power, or could have revealed to me the extent of my spiritual bondage.'

'And have you found the peace you have so long sought?' I inquired.

'Oh, yes', was the response; 'while looking at Jesus, and his infinite worth, before I knew it I was all aglow with love, and found my peace with him.'

Ten years elapsed: years of constant suffering to the poor invalid, which sometimes threw its shadow over her religious life—years, too, of struggle with the old habit, into which she would drift in seasons of temptation and darkness. But she had learned the great secret of Christian joy and strength; and how to come out from herself to lean upon the Savior's bosom. Within a recent period the Master called for her, and she passed away from earth, with perfect trust in a Redeemer's grace, and with a sweet testimony of his love in her heart.

Readers! The story is rich in its suggestions, but I leave it to point its own moral.

9

How It Turns Out Differently [10]

A VESSEL at sea is sometimes caught in the cap of a storm, lurches heavily upon her side, until she dips her spars in the brine, and cannot right herself, but by parting with yards and mast, which she yields—a prey to the tempest. It is no inapt illustration of the sorrows which often burst over the Christian, in the full expansion of his prosperity, before he can reef the affections too incautiously spread before the gale. In the first cup of severe grief, he feels as though he were suddenly lost, when, in reality, he is but thrown from his balance. In the first confusion of his spirit he utters impatient words at that providence which has caught him up, and tosses him fiercely in the fury of the whirlwind. It is in the sober after-thought he 'remembers the years of the right hand of the Most High', and in penitent retraction, exclaims, 'This is my infirmity!' What child of God has not recalled, with pious grief, his hasty impeachment of

[10] Appeared in the *Southwestern Presbyterian,* July 1, 1869.

divine providence, with hearty confession, in the issue, that 'God's thoughts are not his thoughts'? The simple incident, now to be recorded, will afford a double commentary upon this text.

That fearful scourge of the young—the scarlet fever—had laid its iron grip upon a bright boy of eight summers. A dark mahogany band around the throat evinced the fierceness of the assault, under which the helpless victim was throttled. The last sad offices of religion were soon recited at 'little Bennie's' grave, and then came the unavailing service of condolence with the distracted mother. Every topic of conversation was exhausted. Acknowledging God's right to reclaim the life he had given, as an act of mere sovereignty, and freely confessing to its righteousness, as an act simply of retributive justice, she could see no love in the blight which had fallen upon her beautiful boy. In that hour of turbulence her faith could not accept the discipline through which our heavenly Father discloses the wisdom of his love. When urged to wait a little upon God for the interpretation of his purpose, who so often veils his richest blessings under this disguise, the bruised heart could find no solace in what was so contingent; and Rachel wept, and refused to be comforted.

At length, to put the case as concretely as possible, it was suggested—'What if the Lord should, through this bereavement, win your husband to himself? Is he not more to you than ten sons?'

The drooping eye sparkled, like the diamond, in the dew of its own tears, as she replied: 'Ah! if it could be so!

I could see infinite love in that, and kneel with thanksgiving upon the grave of my child, through whom the father was begotten unto God.'

'Madam, God makes no bargains', was the response, 'but trust him with a generous submission, whose promise is: "at evening time it shall be light".'

It was only a hypothesis uttered to show how God could bring good out of evil, and with no expectation of its being an unconscious prophecy.

Three weeks later, like Nicodemus of old, under the cover of darkness, came this husband to that pastor's study. He was a quiet man, moving softly upon his own path, and jostling against no one. Singularly reticent and undemonstrative, what he thought and felt was known only to himself, and to him who reads all hearts. With a faint smile playing around his lips, such as can be seen only when diffidence is breaking through its reserve, he said, 'I am come to tell you that I have found Christ, to whom I have given up my heart.'

Instantly the exclamation burst from me: 'Have you told your wife?'

'No', was the reply; 'only God knows it, and you.'

For the moment I could think of no one but the poor sufferer, whom a few days before I had sought, hypothetically, to console. Had it, then, *turned out so differently* with her who could see nothing but a frown upon her Father's face, when beneath it lay this great joy, which was so soon to drink up all her bitter grief? But recollecting the errand of my visitor, I begged him to tell the whole story of his conversion.

'Sir', he began, 'do you remember saying, some months ago, in a sermon, that God often used affliction as the means by which to draw sinners to himself? In my folly I thought how idle an experiment it would be with me, that if the Almighty should, in that way challenge to a measurement of will against will, it would be seen that something besides coercion would be required to subdue me into a Christian. But, somehow, when little Bennie died, it *turned out very differently.* All this haughty pride was subdued. Instead of this rebellion, I felt strangely drawn to that great Being who had laid upon me this stroke. I have been praying to him ever since, and now I hope that I am at peace with him, through the merits of his Son.'

A long evening was spent in conversation with him, with the most satisfactory conviction that 'old things had passed away', and that he was 'a new creature in Christ Jesus'.

The next day I met, as usual, the Bible-class of ladies, and there, in deep mourning, sat the bereaved mother, with the same dark shadow of grief resting upon the quiet face. I scanned it narrowly, but there was no light that I could discover, breaking in, under the edges of that cloud. 'She is ignorant, yet', I said to myself, 'of the Lord's great love to her.' At the close of the exercise she mingled with the throng, and passed beyond the door. I knew then that I would be the bearer to her of a great joy. Following, with rapid steps, I overtook her, fortunately, alone. 'Mrs. H—, has your husband told you anything?'

A deadly pallor spread over a cheek already too pale, while the hand pressed instinctively, to hold the throbbing heart: 'Is there any new sorrow for me to bear?'

Reader, have you ever felt how the heart of a wounded bird beats against the hand of its captor? So was this poor dove trembling with fear in the hand of God; and yet he was her Father, though she knew it not.

'No, my dear madam, not sorrow, but joy', I rejoined. 'Do you remember telling me how you could kneel at Bennie's grave, and thank God for his infinite love in taking him away?'

'Yes, perfectly well', she answered.

'Go home, then, and tell your husband to erect, this night, the family altar; and as you kneel by his side, praise him who turned for you your mourning into dancing; who hast put off your sackcloth, and girded you with gladness.'

'Has God, then, given me my husband?' she asked in a quick breath.

'Yes, madam; your living husband in the stead of your dead son; and, as he will tell you, the living through the dead.'

Briefly reciting the interview of the preceding night, tears rained down her cheeks as she stood beneath the oaks of the shaded street, but they were tears of holy gratitude and joy, mingled with a little penitence, as she recalled her expressions of despondency and gloom. I bid her *adieu,* with the injunction to help her husband break through the diffidence and reserve so characteristic of him, and so to learn from his own lips the reality

of the great change he had undergone. It was an instructive lesson to me, to wait upon the Lord in the midst of
dark dispensations, until he shall make them plain.

10

For What Have I Done, or What Evil Is in My Hand?[11]

ONE of the most curious exhibitions of human perverseness is the causeless resentment against ministers of the gospel, who happen to be made the depositories of religious convictions from which the parties afterwards resile, and of which they grow to be ashamed. It is, however, easily enough explained. The displacency with which such experiences are remembered, is transferred by natural association to those who are cognizant of the painful secret. The shame which is felt on recalling a weakness, kindles into anger against those who have the power to betray it; upon the same principle that a criminal, bearing on his conscience the burden of an undiscovered crime, hates the witness whose testimony he would dread before the tribunal of justice.

[11] Appeared in the *Southwestern Presbyterian*, July 15, 1869.

It is a peril to which all faithful ministers are exposed. Prudence often restrains the manifestations of this lurking hostility, and they move forward in the freedom of pastoral intercourse in happy ignorance of the same. But, sometimes, the hidden sentiment will, by its own violence, burst into view, to their astonishment and grief. An instance of this once happened to the writer, so marked in its features, and so distinctly confessed, that it is worthy of record. It will, at least, interest those readers whose business it is to study the human heart.

The early boyhood of Mr. W——, was spent under the strict discipline of the Scottish church; but, like many others who have chafed in youth under what they construe as a spiritual despotism, upon his arrival in this country he swung clear of all restraints, and became openly irreligious and profane.

The writer's acquaintance with him originated in a summons to attend what was thought to be his dying bed. It was a severe case of typhoid fever, whose slow fires were consuming him by inches. At length, however, the vigor of a strong constitution triumphed over the disease, which gradually wore itself away; and then followed months of slow and weary convalescence. During this long period of weakness and suffering, I became his companion, discharging, to some extent, the office of nurse as well as that of pastor. Hours were spent, every day, at his bedside, stretching, often, far into the night—and it was difficult to break away, either for rest or for attention to other duties. With his increasing exhaustion, he sank into the waywardness and unreasonableness characteristic, almost, of infancy itself.

At the crisis of his disease, and in the near prospect of death, it is not surprising that conscience should place him under arrest. The contrast was so appalling between the religious training of his youth, and the dreadful apostasy of his later years, as to fill him with remorse. Like Esau, he sought, carefully, even with tears, a place for repentance; and many were the intercessions of others, that he might be saved from the second death. He emerged, finally, from this overwhelming distress into a state, not of simple peace, but of ecstasy and joy. Plainly, this was a case of marvelous grace, or of marvelous delusion. Time cleared up the doubt, painfully enough; but had his earthly career then closed, few would have hesitated to receive it as a wonderful instance of death-bed conversion. Through successive weeks his rapture did not abate, and he spoke with unqualified assurance of his conscious acceptance with God. All this stood in such amazing contrast, not only with his antecedent distress, but with his previous godless life, that, if it had been genuine, it would have been a conspicuous illustration of the sovereignty of divine grace. To his urgent request, however, that he might receive the ordinance of the Lord's Supper, a steady refusal was offered; not from any special misgivings then entertained of the reality of his change, but from the general disinclination to use the sacraments as an immediate preparation for death.

'Mr. W—', said the pastor, 'should you recover, your testimony for Christ will be more valuable if given in the full possession of all your faculties, and not under the restraint of mortal sickness. If you should die, you will be where these ordinances are not needed. There is danger, perhaps, that you would rely too much upon the external sacrament, while your salvation turns upon a naked faith in the Savior himself.'

The result proved this decision to be judicious. It is painful to record that, when the apprehension of death had passed away, and convalescence become established, this pious enthusiasm began to cool, and subsided, at length, into almost total indifference. He went forth from that sick chamber a profane scoffer, and lived more profligately than before. And from that hour his heart seemed to overflow with bitterness to the minister who had been associated with all the experience of that long illness, and whose only offence was that of being the wit- ness of broken vows. Like the venom from a serpent's tooth, he poured forth denunciation and abuse upon one who had showed him nothing but kindness. But this constant defamation being impotent of harm where both the parties were fully known, could the more easily be forgiven as the cause of this revulsion of feeling was so perfectly understood. It excited no other emotions than those of grief and pity, and was never noticed in any form.

After the lapse of about a year, as he was passing, one morning, the pastor's study, he was invited, kindly in; a sealed document was placed in his hands, with this explanation: 'Here, Mr. W——, is your Will, which, you remember, I signed, one year ago, as a witness, and then received from you in trust, to be opened after your death, which you thought to be near at hand. You are now well, and have the prospect of living many years; as you may desire to make important changes in this instrument, I return it to your keeping.'

He received it in silence, whilst I proceeded to remind him of the vows he had made in his hour of danger; the prayers he had offered, and the hopes he had indulged. I placed, solemnly and pointedly, before him, the guilt of his present course, and warned him that God might, at the last, refuse him the opportunity to repent, by destroying him, suddenly, and that without remedy. To this earnest and pungent appeal he listened without a word of reply, but turned away in great rage. The climax of his resentment was reached; his vituperations were, if possible, more bitter than before, until, from the exhaustion of sheer impotence, they at length ceased.

Time rolled on, and these incidents were almost lost in the shadows of the retreating years, when I was, a second time, summoned to Mr. W—'s sick bed. There he lay, with limbs frightfully swollen with dropsy. Extending both hands as I entered, 'I was afraid you would not come, seeing how long I have abused you.'

'I know, too well', I replied, 'the cause of your dislike, to feel anything but the deepest pity for you, Mr. W—.'

'It was conscience, sir, nothing but conscience, all the time. I never believed a word of all I ever said against you; but I never could think of you but as the avenger of my sins, and so I hated the very sight of you.'

'Not an *avenger*, Mr. W—', I rejoined; 'remember who has said, "Vengeance is mine; I will repay, saith

63

the Lord"; but a *witness* I am obliged to be of vows most solemnly taken, and alas! most profanely broken.'

'I know it all, too well, my dear friend', was the answer, 'for it burns like a dreadful fire, just here', laying his hand upon his heart.

'God is infinitely merciful', I replied, 'and you are alive to pray for pardon, which you know is a greater privilege than I supposed God would ever offer you again.'

'It is more than I deserve; God grant it may be a token of mercy in store for me, that he gives me another sick bed's opportunity.'

The story need not be drawn out in its details, suffice it to say that he lingered through months of suffering, during which I constantly attended him. He seemed to be thoroughly penitent and subdued, and died, at last expressing a quiet trust in the merits of Jesus Christ. There was not, however, an approach to the rapture he had expressed under like circumstances, before. But, so far as man could judge, there was less hazard of mistake than then. He was more humble, and had a deeper sense of the deceitfulness of sin, and prayed, with apparent fervor, that he might be preserved from a false hope, and so repeat the crime of his first illness. It was difficult to bring myself to the same confidence in him that I once had; but I laid him down to his rest, in the hope that he had truly passed from death to life, and was numbered among the saints, in glory.

There is one point of special interest in the fore-going narrative, to which reference will be made in a subsequent paper. The case is recited, now, simply to illustrate how innocently a faithful minister may fall under the displeasure of wicked men. 'The carnal mind is enmity against God', says the apostle; is it strange that it should sometimes turn, in a side-wise direction, against those who are identified with his cause, and are viewed as the exponents of his cause? Let not such, therefore, be amazed, if they are involved in Christ's reproach, but remember his word of faithful forewarning: 'If the world hate you, you know that it hated me before it hated you. The servant is not greater than his Lord: if they have persecuted me, they will also persecute you; if they have kept my saying, they will keep yours, also.'

11

Clinic Administration of the Sacraments[12]

IN a preceding paper[13] reference was made to a case in which the Lord's Supper was refused to one in the near prospect of death. This approached as near a test case as can well be imagined. Not only did the party profess faith and repentance, but his hope mounted into joyful assurance of pardon and acceptance with God. All this experience was afterwards shown to be spurious, and was followed by a fearful apostasy. But at the moment no misgivings were entertained, and it was regarded as a conspicuous illustration, both of the sovereignty and freeness of divine grace.

The question now arises whether, under this aspect, it was right to withhold the ordinance so greatly desired. Every pastor is interested in the reply, for similar cases

[12] Appeared in the *Southwestern Presbyterian,* July 22, 1869.
[13] No. 10, p. 58.

are constantly occurring in our intercourse with the sick and the dying, in which the strongest appeals are made to our natural sympathies, and in which, on that account, there is the more need of established principles for our guidance.

On the one hand, if, according to our catechism, a sacrament is a 'holy ordinance, instituted by Christ, wherein, by sensible signs, Christ and the benefits of the new covenant are represented, sealed, and applied to believers', there seems no reason why it should not be administered to one on his deathbed who, for the first time, gives credible evidence of a change of heart. If, upon that same evidence, he would, in health, be received into the church, and be admitted to sealing ordinances, what is there in the simple circumstance that he is at the gates of the eternal world to debar him of the enjoyment of this high privilege? Nay, we can readily sympathize with the desire such a person might feel, to recover, as far as possible, the wasted opportunities of the past, and by the most solemn profession of his faith, to leave his dying testimony on behalf of that Savior, whom he has neglected all his life. Were this the only aspect of the case, and no disturbing element interposed to mar the conclusion, we should only require reasonable proof of the reality of a spiritual change to warrant the application of the covenant seal.

On the other hand, if the sacraments are intended to subserve other and collateral ends, of 'obliging believers to obedience', of 'testifying their love and communion, one with another', and of 'distinguishing them from those that are without', this private and clinic administration seems to be, at least, *aside* from the object for which they were instituted. They were given as social ordinances to the church, in her present militant state, and presuppose the recipient to be in a condition to render the service to which he is herein engaged, and of witnessing a good confession before the world, from which he is hereby discriminated. What opportunity has one, at the very end of life, of verifying, by his obedience, the reality of his conversion, or of holding fellowship with the godly, when the solitary act left to be performed is simply to die, and thus to pass away from the scenes for which these sacraments were obviously intended?

A still more appalling difficulty presents itself in the dreadful perversion of the sacraments by those who advocate the doctrine of 'sacramental grace'. Very early in the history of the church, an exaggerated value began to attach to these 'tremendous mysteries', emerging, at length, into the Romish and Tractarian doctrine, that 'the sacraments contain the grace which they signify or represent, and confer it always upon all who receive them, unless they put a bar or obstacle in the way; and that they confer, or bestow grace thus universally, *ex opere operato*, that is, by some power or virtue given to them, and operating through them'. The legalism of the natural heart clings with frightful tenacity to this fatal opinion of 'an invariable connection between the sacraments, as outward ordinances, and the communication of spiritual blessings'; and that by 'some sort of intrinsic

power, or inherent capacity' in the sacraments themselves. Is it strange, then, that pastors—who are jealous
for the Word of God, and for the blessed Redeemer,
whose glory is taken from him, and carried over to the
institutions which were meant simply to represent and
seal him to the faith of his people—should shrink from
the great responsibility of fostering this fatal delusion
by too easy compliance with the wishes of those who
watch around a dying bed?

The writer's design, however, is not to discuss these
grave principles, so much as to illustrate the embarrassment which a conscientious minister often feels in
dealing with cases in which they are involved.

In exemplification of the peril in complying too
readily with the desire of sick persons to receive these
ordinances, two additional cases may be cited, both falling under his pastoral notice:

Mrs. B— had grown up without enjoying, in childhood, the advantages of religious training. She became
the mother of a large household, and spent a long life
in almost total indifference to the subject of religion,
except that she paid to it the outward respect of waiting
upon the ministry of the Word. This apathy did not
yield till near the close of her last illness, from a chronic
disease which was slow in working to its issue, and
during whose weary continuance, her pastor dealt with
her conscience in great plainness and fidelity. Through
a long season of darkness and doubt she emerged, at last,
into a sustaining hope of pardon—but a hope which
always remained obscure and trembling. Her friends,

who belonged, chiefly, to another branch of the church, urged upon her the importance of the sacrament of the Supper, as a preparation for death, before a full exposition, however, of the views held by us. She acquiesced in them, and only on one occasion manifested undue solicitude on the subject. One Sabbath morning, at breakfast, the pastor was hastily summoned to her bedside. She thought the crisis of her disease rapidly approaching; and as he entered her chamber she greeted him with this most affecting appeal: 'Do you, as a minister of the gospel, and acquainted with its holy teachings, feel perfectly sure that I can go to heaven without the sacrament?' The reply was:

'Whatever doubt, my dear madam, I may have before had of the propriety of withholding that ordinance, is canceled by your question. With its sound ringing in my ear, I would cut off my hand before I would administer it to you. Christ Jesus is the only Savior; the true kindness is to shut you up to a naked faith in him, and to allow nothing, not even his most blessed memorial ordinance, to come in between your faith and him.'

'I am perfectly satisfied', was her answer, sinking back upon her pillow. 'My friends have urged it, so that I was a little shaken with fear lest some thing necessary might be left undone; but I prefer to trust myself to your guidance than to theirs.'

She died, after a few weeks, in peace, and the subject was never re-opened. Yet the case brought down no small reproach upon the pastor, as guilty of the most arbitrary and wanton cruelty.

Upon another occasion the writer was sent for, in the middle of the night, to administer baptism to a gentleman, supposed to be near his end. It was a severe and prolonged attack of typhoid fever, accompanied by the stupor and deliriousness so characteristic of that disease. In this case, as in the other, the ministering friends were of another church, which attaches more importance to a ritualistic observance of the sacraments that is common amongst Presbyterians. As soon as I entered the chamber and perceived the condition of the patient, I pronounced that he was incompetent for the ordinance. He lay in a heavy lethargy, from which, when aroused, the incoherent utterances betrayed the entire derangement of all the intellectual faculties. A few words of explanation satisfied the parties, who were not unreasonable, that, consistently with our views of what was implied in the baptism of adults, he was wholly incapable of making that profession of personal faith in Christ upon which the administration of the ordinances is based. In the good providence of God, the sufferer survived his disease, and upon his recovery solemnly assured the writer that he had no recollection of having asked for baptism, as reported, and that he could not recall any religious emotions, of any kind, at that period of his sickness. He further expressed his thanks that the request had been declined, as he should always have been tormented with doubts of its validity if baptism had been administered, saying, with emphasis, 'Why, sir, it would have been the same thing as though you had baptized a log.'

It is pleasant to add that he subsequently united with the church, upon a profession made in the possession of all his mental powers, and that he lives, at this day, an ornament and a pillar in the house of God.

Instances of this kind, of almost daily occurrence in pastoral experience, suggest the caution with which these sealing ordinances of the church should be dispensed to persons drawing near to death, and as a preparation for that momentous change. Of course, these remarks are not intended to touch the case of bedridden saints, whom physical infirmities debar from attendance upon the sanctuary. It is both common and proper on Sacramental Sabbaths, to bear the elements to the chambers of such as, being of the household of faith, and constructively present with the great congregation, as they engage in this act of joint communion. The point against which this *caveat* is written is the disposition to construe the Lord's Supper as a species of extreme unction, *sacramentum exeuntium*, by which all that is suspicious and defective in a late death-bed repentance, shall be overtaken and supplemented. We cannot be too cautious against fostering an error so fatal to salvation, and which, by its misdirection, has probably cut off many a soul which might have found life, had nothing been presented to its view but the cross of Christ.

12

It Shall Not Return unto Me Void—
Isaiah 55:11[14]

THE night of a Communion Sabbath set in with a dark, drizzling rain. The feverish excitement, springing from unusual labor, had just subsided into the light slumber which precedes the deeper rest of the weary, when I was awakened by a carriage rolling over the stones, and pausing at my door. Upon throwing open the casement I found it to be a call to attend a dying man. As the cold wintry wind penetrated my loose robe, upon the balcony, the first feeling was that of impatience at the inopportune and unwelcome summons. In the next instant I was bowed with shame under the rebukes of conscience, at this reluctance to sacrifice present ease to the demands of duty. While making a hurried toilet, a voice of expostulation came from the bed I had just abandoned: 'This is too bad: the night is

14 Appeared in the *Southwestern Presbyterian,* July 29, 1869.

stormy, and you are fatigued; take the address and offer to come early in the morning.'

It was the pleading of a natural but selfish affection that sought to shield from exposure one who was very dear. 'No', was the reply; 'death waits upon no man's convenience, and an immortal soul may be at stake.'

The slanting rain drove past the edge of the half-covered vehicle as I sat down upon the dampened cushions, and was driven through the dim and cheerless streets of the city.

Stopping, at length, before a house, I groped my way, by an obscure staircase, into the sick man's chamber, when, to my utter amazement, he exclaimed—stretching out both his hands to greet me: 'I am so glad that you have come; I have sent for you to pray with me, but chiefly to tell you that I die in the comfortable hope of salvation, to which I have been led through your instrumentality.'

Was it for this the loving Lord had roused me from my slumber, to administer this cordial to his repining servant? How much more deeply the rebuke sank upon the conscience, for its very tenderness and grace! I could have wept, had I been alone, for the half-resentment with which I had chafed but a few moments before; when the Good Master only meant to place in my hands, and that before the judgment day, the record of my work. There was not time, however, for private reflections of this sort, profitable as they might be.

The sick man resumed, 'I have led a reckless and wicked life, free from all restraints of religion or of virtue. In a disreputable calling, which associated me with the vicious and profane, I had long since forgotten all the pious instructions of my childhood; indulging every appetite, and gratifying every passion of a depraved nature. But six months ago I stumbled, by what then seemed to me only an accident, into your church. It was night, and I was attracted by the brilliant lights, and sat down in the gallery at your left hand. Your text was, "Come, and let us reason together, saith the Lord; though your sins be as scarlet, they shall be as white as snow; though they be red, like crimson, they shall be as wool." Do you remember, sir, preaching from those words?'

'Perfectly well', I answered; 'and could give you, now, the outlines of the discourse, if it were necessary.'

'Well, sir, those precious words of Scripture shot through and through me, as you repeated them. I thought I had never heard anything so beautiful; and they seemed so exactly suited to me, whose sins were just the scarlet and the crimson there described. As you went on expounding and enforcing them, I drank up every word with a strange wonder and delight, that there was such a gospel and such a Savior for such a sinner as myself. Ever since that night I have been a new man, and have never lost a single sermon you have preached, until about two weeks ago, when I was taken with this pneumonia, which is carrying me to the grave.'

'How was it', I asked, 'you never told me all this before? I would have been so happy to have taught you the way of the Lord more perfectly.'

'I can hardly tell you why I did not, except that I had always lived in such a different world from you, and could never get the courage to break over the barrier which separated us. Besides, everything was dark and confused to me, but this, that God, through Christ, could make my sins as snow. But, now that I am dying, I could not rest till I had told you how I have hanging upon those precious words, and how happy I feel now in the hope that they are fulfilled in me.'

I was too thoroughly subdued and melted to leave this new-found friend that night. All exhaustion and weariness had fled in the exhilaration of the draught which the adorable Savior placed then to my lips. I knelt and prayed with a fervor inspired by gratitude to him who had shown such mercy to this poor sufferer and to me. I rose from my knees only to open more fully the infinite riches of that grace, of which he had obtained the first great hint. In this religious communion the night wore away, interrupted only by the last directions left to the friends, who ministered about him, as to the disposal of his worldly effects. At length, amid the small hours beyond twelve, he gently sank to sleep, resting in the arms of that divine Savior whom he seemed to have embraced with almost childhood's simple faith.

In the gray of the morning I threaded my way through the dripping streets, pondering the words of Scripture: 'In the morning sow thy seed, and in the evening withhold not thine hand, for thou knowest not whether shall prosper, either this or that, or whether they shall both be alike good', and at the same time rejoicing that it takes so little truth to save a soul, when it is applied by the Holy Spirit, and received in the simplicity of faith.

13

Practical Uses of
the Doctrine of Inability [15]

DURING the first year of my ministry, a young friend, in whom I was particularly interested, came to spend a week with me, before his entrance upon college life. By a good providence his visit was happily timed, for it happened to be a season of 'refreshing from the presence of the Lord', chiefly under the labors of that eminent evangelist, the Rev. Dr. J. C. Stiles. Christians were aroused, and many were awakened to seek the salvation of their souls. Preaching had been continued every night for several weeks, and prayer meetings were held at such hours of the day as interfered least with those secular duties which, in their proper season, true religion directs and sanctifies as much as our acts of devotion.

My young friend seemed annoyed at finding this state of things, and had scarcely exchanged greetings with us

[15] Appeared in the *Southwestern Presbyterian,* August 5, 1869.

before he said, 'You are so busy here with meetings that I believe I will return home tomorrow.'

'No', was the reply; 'you came to spend a week, and a week you must stay. The meetings need not trouble you a particle, if you are disinclined to attend them.' In this he finally acquiesced; but as the alternative was to remain in the house, alone, or accompany us to church, it ended in his being a constant attendant upon the night services, amusing himself with the books of my library during my brief absence during the day. I was cautious not to press the subject of religion upon him, in private, but strove, simply, to make his visit agreeable by the most free and unreserved intercourse with him upon ordinary topics. It was clear that he was under considerable irritation of spirits, like one caught in a snare, and that his stay was prolonged merely through civility, and a regard to our feelings.

Thus matters moved on from day to day, till the Sabbath came and was passed; and on Monday the conflict reached its crisis. I was waiting in my study as he came in and sat beside my desk—breaking out, after a little, in the petulant remark: 'You preachers are the most contradictory men in the world; you say, and you unsay, just as it pleases you, without the least pretension to consistency.'

Somehow I was not surprised at this outbreak; for, though no sign of religious feeling had been evinced, there was a restlessness in his manner which satisfied me that he was secretly fighting against the truth. I thought it best to treat the case in an off-hand sort of way, and with seeming indifference, so as to cut him off from all opportunity to coquet with the gospel. Without arresting my pen, I simply answered, 'Well, what now?'

'Why, yesterday, you said in your sermon that sinners were perfectly helpless in themselves—utterly unable to repent or to believe, and then turned square round and said that they would all be damned if they did not.'

'Well, my dear E——, there is no use in our quarreling over this matter; either you can, or you can not; if you can, all I have to say is that I hope you will just go and do it.'

As I did not raise my eyes from my writing, which was continued, as I spoke, I had no means of marking the effect of these words, until, after a moment's silence, with a choking utterance, the reply came back:

'I have been trying my best for three whole days, and cannot.'

'Ah', said I, laying down the pen; 'that puts a different face upon it; we will go, then, and tell the difficulty straight out to God.'

We knelt together, and I prayed in the most matter-of-fact style, as though this was the first time in human history this trouble had ever arisen; that here was a soul in the most desperate extremity, which must believe or perish, and hopelessly unable, of itself, to do it; that, consequently, it was just the case calling for divine interposition; and pleading most earnestly for the fulfillment of the divine promise. Upon rising I offered not a single word of comfort or advice. Youth is seldom disingenuous or stubborn, and the difficulty was recognized as purely practical. So I left my friend, in his powerlessness, in the hands of God, as the only helper. In a short time he came through the struggle, rejoicing in the hope of eternal life.

It is only necessary to add, as the sequel of the story, that he passed, successfully, through the temptations of a collegiate career; became, in due season, a divinity student; and is now, after the lapse of twenty years, an honored and useful minister of that gospel whose power to save he then first felt.

The fact simply is, that 'the carnal mind is enmity against God—for it is not subject to the law of God; neither, indeed, *can* be.' The danger is not so much that the sinner will be crushed into despair by the clear apprehension of this truth, as that he will fail to realize it at all. They wrap themselves in the fatal delusion that they are competent to repent at will, and so they sport with the whole matter as being perfectly under their control. The issue becomes fearfully momentous, as soon as they practically discover that they are, in themselves, utterly without strength, and, therefore, wholly dependent upon the sovereign mercy of God. It is unwise to strip the truth of the apparent sternness by any attempts at metaphysical explanation, or to blunt its edge by offering premature comfort. It is better to deal honestly with it as a tremendous fact, and then leave the awakened sinner face to face with his great peril, thrown back in this solemn crisis upon the pledged mercy of God, in Christ. '"Shall I bring to the birth, and not cause to bring forth?" saith the Lord.'

Another illustration of the practical efficiency of this, and allied doctrines, is furnished in the history of a gentleman who, for many years, sat upon my left hand, immediately beneath the pulpit. There he writhed, Sabbath after Sabbath, under these distasteful yet wholesome truths, and sent me frequent messages that if I did not stop those 'prosy doctrinal sermons', he would quit the church. I knew better. I knew the fascination of the truth, when it has once caught the conscience with its eye, and that the sinner's torture is that he is about as impotent to bolt away from it as to accept it in the simplicity of faith. 'Prosy doctrines', forsooth; why I could pour down from that pulpit a cataract of appeals, awful as Niagara, with all its thunders, without stirring a pulse in his heart; but if I pointed my finger, ever so quietly, and said, in effect, 'Mr. F—, you are a lost soul if God, in his sovereign mercy, does not help you to trust in Christ', the man would quiver in every nerve. At last, God's hand was laid upon him in bereavement and bodily suffering. 'Ah', said now the softened spirit, 'I used to hate those doctrines of yours, for they tore me up by the roots. I would be mad with you every Sabbath, and swear that I would never hear another sermon, but the next Sabbath would find me back in the pew. But, oh! those old doctrines, cold and hard, like steel, which had no compromises about them; they frightened me more than all the pictures of hell you ever drew.'

I replied: 'Mr. F—, you need not explain anything of that to me. I have read your heart, just like a printed book, these five years past, down and up, and cross-wise, inside and out, for I have been all through that mill myself, and know every wheel and pulley in it. The harpoon went into your side long ago, and the Lord has been paying out the rope these five years to you, and you have spouted up barrels of water, and made the sea red with your blood. But now he is pulling in the rope, and very soon you will be one of the sweetest captives the gospel ever had.'

And so it proved, conscience and the truth triumphed, perfectly, over prejudice and wrath; and for years he sealed a quiet testimony for the grace of God, by a pious life, and at last, by a peaceful and happy death.

There is, at last, no preaching so efficacious as the calm, sober, discriminating statement of the doctrines of grace, uttered with all that tenderness springing from a full conviction of their absolute truth, and of their transcendent importance. There is, consequently, no fallacy greater than to distinguish between doctrinal and practical preaching, to the disparagement of the former. 'Truth is in order to godliness'; and the clear exposition and enforcement of the doctrines of the Bible is worth, infinitely, more that all the bold exhortation which rant has uttered, since the time of Noah.

PART TWO

Thoughts upon
Foreign Missions

14

Thoughts upon Foreign Missions—No. 1 [1]

EARTHLY conquerors, in the spirit of gasconade, have babbled of universal dominion. But their world has turned out to mean only a larger or a smaller section of the earth's surface; whilst the rapidity with which these crazy empires of the sword have disintegrated, attests the truth that nothing is weaker than what men call force. But the conception of an empire which shall belt the globe, and blend into harmony all the jarring tongues of men; which shall establish the supremacy of reason over passion, and of conscience over wrong; the reign of goodness and love, swaying all hearts by the power of truth—this is one of those divine thoughts, like that of incarnation and redemption, throbbing only in the pages of the Bible.

We should expect the splendid suggestion to touch the chord of bravery in every Christian breast, and that

[1] Appeared in the *Southwestern Presbyterian,* March 4, 1869.

life and treasure would flow like water beneath the standard of the cross, in this aggressive warfare. But, alas! the haze, which hangs over all things that are grand on earth, dims the glory of this kingdom to many eyes; and faith overtakes, with laggard steps, what is desired only in the prophetic future. The sympathy which is stirred by the near, languishes before the distant; and the enthusiasm of the church cools into indifference, if it does not harden into opposition. The apparent fruitlessness of past efforts, for example, is adduced in evidence that the whole enterprise is wild and chimerical. What, it is asked, has been accomplished, after the stupendous efforts of nearly two thousand years, beyond simply transferring Christianity from one quarter of the globe to another? If the church shall continue to recede in one direction as far as she advances in another, what hope may be cherished of her universal triumph? And if, at this late day, three-fourths of the human race remain to be evangelized, how many cycles will be required before those sublime prophecies shall be fulfilled?

To this objection, stated here in its full force, we reply, distinctly, as follows:

1. *It proves too much.* Here, in our own Christian land, where the gospel is proclaimed from thousands of pulpits, it would not be extravagant to estimate that one-half of our gross population escapes from its control. With the powerful aid of a religious press; with a public Christian sentiment bearing down with the silent and constant pressure of the atmosphere; with religious institutions, entrenched within the protection of the civil law, how

small a proportion of souls who really bow before the scepter of our King! Subtract the multitudes who never come beneath the shadow of the sanctuary, and then deduct those who wait upon its ordinances, without the profession of godliness, and the small residuum is the meager roll of such as, in the judgment of charity, may be reckoned the true subjects of the cross. How easily, then, might the infidel retort this language of Christian despondency upon the church at home? Your religion, he cries, is proved a failure; if, after these vast appliances, the overwhelming majority tramples upon it with such disdainful rejection. Do you reply:- This only proves the desperate enmity of the natural heart against God, and the severity of that conflict between sin and holiness which must go on to the bitter end in this wretched world? Why shall not this be more intensely true of heathen lands, where this native depravity is reinforced by the prescription of ancient customs; by the sanctity of hoary superstitions; by the power of social caste; and by all the influence of government and laws arrayed against a new and thoroughly subversive system of thought and worship? In point of fact the objection, in either case, misconceives the purpose of God in the proclamation of his truths, which, wherever it goes, at home and abroad, will find out and win to Christ, his own elect. His Word will not return to him void, either here or there. It is carried just where His redeemed are to be found; and the fact that they are there, is determined by the presence of that gospel through which they are to be saved. Paul must remain eighteen months at Corinth because of the 'much people' whom the Lord had there. And the missionary treads the shores of India or China with the assurance of the same fact. If, then, the Christian would not dismantle the sanctuary and disband the ministry at home, nor silence the voice of the Bible in his own land, let him not whisper a secret to the skeptic, by which the very batteries of Christianity may be turned against his own fortresses.

2. *The agency of Missions may be an ordained method of preserving Christianity upon the earth.* This thought is intended to parry the complaint that the church has done little more, in two thousand years, but shift her seat from one continent to another. But suppose the church, in Apostolic times, had locked herself within the limits of Palestine, who can pronounce how far her destruction might have been involved in the total overthrow of the Jewish nationality? Or, suppose the interests of all Christendom had been deposited with the churches of the Reformation in France and Spain, who can tell whether they would not have perished in the almost complete extinction of those churches in the fires of persecution? If Rome had but one neck, the insane wish of Nero had been realized—of placing his foot at once upon the life of a whole people. The wisdom of God seems to provide against this 'peril' by so diffusing his church that she is safe from those contingencies which sometimes overwhelm a single state in hopeless ruin.

Again: Heresies and corruptions spring up in the bosom of the church herself, and she rolls down the swift declension towards utter apostasy. If restrained within narrow boundaries, she is in danger of being suffocated by the false philosophy and science in which the thought of an entire nation is sometimes steeped. Witness the rationalism of Germany, today, which, but two centuries ago, was the cradle and bulwark of the Reformation. Nothing could be more profusely illustrated from the history of the past than this. When Gnosticism threatened to poison the theology of the Asiatic church, this developed itself in the different mold of Grecian thought. When again about to evaporate in the metaphysical subtleties of the Alexandrian School, it found refuge in the robust and practical life of Latin Christianity. When the whole Roman Empire subsided beneath the flood of Gothic invasion, the church transferred her treasures to the shores of England, to the forests of Germany, and to the mountains of Switzerland. Hidden there for ten centuries, she burst from her concealment in the vigor and piety of the great Reformation. When overlaid in Europe by the restrictions of state alliance, she spread her broad wing over intervening oceans, and made a new history for herself in the cabins and chapels of this Western world. In short, Christianity must have its own historical outworking in all generations and in all lands. It must pass through all the possible forms of human thought, and feel the 'pressure' of every actual condition of society. Then, gathering up in her grasp all of human experience and knowledge, she may, with the accumulated force, roll back over the path she has once traveled, and repossess the regions which she only seems to abandon.

3. *Missionary statistics silence this complaint of fruitlessness by showing precisely the reverse.* Upon no department of Christian labor has the seal of God's blessing been more signally placed. If in one region of the globe a longer time is spent in breaking up the fallow ground, the harvest gathered has usually been proportioned to the delay. The time is not lost in trenching the soil, if a richer culture yields a more abundant return. In the sphere of providence no one waits upon God, in the patient use of appointed means, without a reward. And, preeminently, is this true in the kingdom of grace—the very constitution of which, provides for the free development of every virtue springing out of the divine life with which a believing soul is impregnated. As to the success of missionary labor, what favored pastor at home would not gratefully present the record of six or seven hundred souls brought to Christ, and united to the church, during a ministry of fifteen years? Yet we have just been told this summary of the labors of Rev. Alfred Wright, among the Choctaw Indians, after his settlement at Wheelock. Or, if the comparison is wanted upon a broader scale, examine the records of the missions among the Pacific Isles; or the labors of the Moravians, everywhere; and with all the advantages possessed by us at home, no one of us can boast against his brother, standing alone amidst the wastes of heathenism; to whom the Lord whispers, pointing to a group of native converts: 'This shall be a token unto thee that I have sent thee.'

4. *The duty of the church, in this particular, turns upon no considerations of human policy.* The evangelization of the

globe may be difficult—nay, if you please, to human judgment, impracticable. But what place is there for these things in a kingdom that is confessed supernatural? The regeneration of a single soul, under the best auspices, demands the exercise of infinite power. The salvation of a hemisphere can exact nothing higher. The question of duty is to be settled then, upon other principles quite, than either the speculative judgments, or even the recorded experience of men. The work is ours—the success is his who has enjoined it. Is it not by this that the faith, little as the mustard seed, casts mountains into the sea; and that paralytics stretch forth, in simple obedience, the withered hand?

We greatly fear that in the folds of this objection is coiled a fearful skepticism, as to the truth of God. Hath he not said it, not as of a thing yet in the future, but contemplated as past—done: 'the kingdoms of this world are become the kingdoms of our Lord and of Christ?' Yea, let God be true, and every whisper of distrust and unbelief be silenced forever. If an honorable man resents, with quickest jealousy, the impeachment of his veracity, how much more the great God, who 'is not a man that he should lie, nor the son of man that he should repent?'

15

Thoughts upon
Foreign Missions—No. 2 [2]

A MORE common objection against foreign missions
is drawn from the destitutions which remain to be
overtaken in our own land. In the terse language of Mr.
Randolph, 'the Greeks are at our doors,' why should
the energies of the church be scattered abroad, when
the utmost concentration is imperiously demanded at
home? For the most part, this plea is a simple invasion,
sufficiently manifest in being the utterance of those who
are shamefully recreant to the very duty which they so
vehemently urge. Were it not for a class of sincere but
narrow Christians, besides them, who are beguiled by
this sophistry, from a due consideration of their obligations to the heathen, it would not be worth while to
enter upon its articulate discussion.

[2] Appeared in *Southwestern Presbyterian,* March 11, 1869.

'A man convinced against his will, is of the same opinion still' and no style of argument will carry conviction to one whose sole endeavor is to escape from responsibility. But candid minds may possibly be recovered from prejudices by which they have been unfortunately warped. It is to such alone the following considerations are adapted:

I. *One plain duty cannot displace or cancel another.* 'This ought you to have done, and not to leave the other undone.' The principle is so obvious as scarcely to admit of expansion, and yet it is amazing in how many directions it is completely overturned. It is a great deal better to dance, say the lovers of pleasure, than to talk scandal; most assuredly, but we fail to perceive the alternative: why do either? It is better to steal than to kill; perhaps so, we do not deny a gradation in crime: but the same law forbids both. The apology is often offered for the poor inebriate: he is a foe to no one but himself: yet there are high and solemn obligations under which a man lies to himself, and he is a great offender who tramples even upon them. Does it require long reflection to discover how this hollow reasoning cancels every duty in its turn, and in the destruction of all morality takes society to pieces by the joint? The question of evangelizing the nations of the earth is very little affected by any comparison we may institute with other and coordinate obligations. It is to be determined upon far different principles than the views we may chance to entertain of its relative importance. Do the heathen need the gospel as the only means through which they can be saved? Does it lie in the very frame and constitution of the gospel, that it is intended for the human race, and is the property of no privileged class? Still more clearly: Is it the direct and positive command of our King that we shall bear his message of reconciliation to all the world? If so, then the duty is plain, and cannot be jostled out of its place by any other duty, however important. There may be junctures in which the claims of our own country may be particularly urgent, as at this moment in the suffering and dismantled South; yet it never can be otherwise than that, 'Beginning at Jerusalem, repentance and remission of sins shall be preached among all nations.'

2. *The objection postpones indefinitely the world's conversion.* When will this pressure upon the home field be so far relieved that the undivided energies of the church may be thrown out upon foreign enterprise? As well may we ask when a great city will be so far finished that the sound of the builder's hammer shall not disturb the repose of its sleeping inhabitants. Never will the time come, in the most favored portions of Christendom, when the testimonial spire will point to heaven in every retired hamlet; when no feeble church shall anywhere depend upon charitable aid; when the outcast shall not need to be gathered into new folds from the hedges and the lanes where they now wander as sheep without a shepherd. If the Lord has a faithful seed to serve him in any country, rest assured there will always be the seed of the serpent to confront them in bitter warfare. The church will never see her work done, nor her conflict

ended, at any point on the surface of the globe; and to suspend her efforts for the salvation of the heathen until this be accomplished is, in parliamentary phrase, but a motion for its indefinite postponement. It would be more truthful and manly to decline the Lord's work outright, than to escape from it by an indirection of this sort; to say to the heathen, in plain terms, they must perish in their guilt, without the gospel, than to hold up a false hope of distant relief, which the lapse of ages will never redeem. If the deadly opiate were ever withheld, perhaps the Christians' conscience would rouse from its torpor, and the great work be done at last with something of solemn earnestness.

3. *Consider the reflex influences of an expansive charity,* which embraces the world in its scope, in redoubling the zeal of Christians at home. In fact, the two are not antagonistic, but correlative. It is one work, spreading in concentric circles, just as a stone, thrown upon the bosom of a lake, throws out rings which widen till they strike, on every side, the opposing shore. It is precisely against the schismatical tendencies of this objection, breaking up into parts that which is really one, we so urgently protest. Imbue the church with the idea that the preaching of the gospel in the domestic field only presses out the borders of that enclosure which is to embrace at last the most distant tribes of the earth; and there will be a vast accession of power from the grandeur of the scale upon which her efforts are projected. It is the return stroke of the lightning which is most effective; and the charity which yearns over the heathenism of Asia, will be strangely inconsistent

with itself if it does not return with intense longing to repair the desolations of America.

Who does not know the power of a great principle to rouse the dormant energies of the soul, and put it upon superhuman achievements? Every true hero is made such by the force of some exalted purpose, which takes possession of the heart, and swallows up every thing foreign to itself. The glow of enthusiasm is felt through the entire being, which, by its kindling warmth, melts down every force of opposition; and a lofty courage bears the conqueror through every peril, until complete success shall throw around his head the halo of its own glory. Such a purpose, not great, simply, but God-like, is that of the world's conquest for Christ. The heart, of which it takes full possession, is made heroic. And if nothing less will satisfy its ambition than the *whole* world, how shall not this include the home evangelization? The eye, which at the center sweeps around the circumference of the circle, takes within its range every object which that circle encloses; and the sympathy which rests upon the heathen, afar off, will weep and work for the more guilty heathen at our own door. This explains the well-known fact that all who are foremost in their zeal for foreign missions, are foremost in the propagation of the gospel in their own land. Show us a single heart, earnest for the conversion of the Gentiles, which is lukewarm to the progress of Christianity at home, and we will show hundreds indifferent to the heathen who never bestow an effort upon their neighbors at their side. In reality, all the schemes of evangelization, both at home and abroad, are sustained by the liberality and the toil of exactly the same persons.

4. We disallow the objections, upon the ground that *it works a forfeiture of the divine blessing upon the church in our own land.* It is needless to remind the reader how entirely the efficiency of the pulpit depends upon the co-operating agency of the Holy Spirit: 'we have this treasure in earthen vessels, that the excellency of the power may be of God, and not of us.' The highest gifts are exercised in vain, without the intervention of divine power. Paul may plant and Apollos may water, but it is God who giveth the increase. And the seed, buried in the soil, 'abideth alone,' except it be warmed into life by the heat of the sun, and be matured by the dews and rain from heaven, so the Word perishes, without fruit, in the human breast, except it be quickened by the brooding energies of the Spirit, to whom the all-saving application of the gospel is officially assigned. How perilous then to trifle with duty and with God, on the part of those who are put in trust with this gospel for the whole world! May it not be well to consider whether there be any more certain way to defeat the best laid plans for the salvation of those around us, than by provoking the Almighty to withhold that blessing upon which the success of all human effort is acknowledged to depend? Through the channels of a universal commerce the gates of all nations are opened to the church; and thus she is summoned by the voice of providence to execute her high commission of bearing the gospel into all lands. She may not shrink from the glorious enterprise, without forfeiting every claim upon the divine favor. We would

not, indeed, presumptuously limit the Holy One of Israel in the exercise of his sovereignty; but the church deals with God through the covenant which he has graciously formed with her, in which privilege and duty are inseparably bound together. A divorce between these dissolves the bonds of the covenant itself, and works the forfeiture of that privilege which is attempted to be seized, without the duty which is its correlate. The entire history of the Church, from the ascension until now, shows that the periods of her greatest purity and power have been the seasons of her aggressive activity; and, conversely, that her days of sloth and ease have been marked by corruption, heresy and schism. 'There is that withholdeth, but it tendeth toward poverty.'

5. This plea is particularly *ungrateful in those who, upon that ground, would never themselves have known the gospel.* Let us suppose that Apostolic Christianity had rested contentedly within the limits of Palestine; or, at furthest, had been satisfied with the territory which it conquered in Asia Minor, and in Greece—what then? Can it be overlooked that, but a few centuries ago, the region we now call Christendom, was the region of heathenish darkness? That the very ancestors of those, who would now lock up the gospel in the countries it has explored, worshiped beneath the oaks of the forest, according to the dark and bloody rites of ancient Druidism? The plea, which is good for our age, is equally good for every other; and upon this principle we, ourselves, had been idolaters of the darkest complexion. Verily, then, we are debtors, in the largest sense, to those portions of the

world from which Christianity was first transmitted to us; and simple gratitude binds us to reciprocate the benefits which, ages since, they conferred. May God, in his infinite mercy, prevent us from sliding, like the churches of the East, into heathenism again, as the punishment of our indifference and sloth—condemned, a second time, to receive the gospel from those who, today, implore it at our hands!

16

Thoughts upon
Foreign Missions—No. 3[3]

THE apathy of the Christian world upon the subject of foreign missions is not sufficiently explained upon either of the two suppositions canvassed in preceding articles. A deeper cause must be found in a secret impression that the heathen may be saved without the knowledge of the gospel. It is not necessary that this thought should translate itself into speech. It exists often as a sentiment, where it is not announced as a doctrine—and is all the more dangerous when thus concealed in the mind. Many would shrink from the responsibility of defending it as an open statement, with a clear perception of its tremendous sweep, and against the whole array of Scripture testimony. But it can lurk in the corners of the soul, diffusing its narcotic influence over all its sensibilities, without being recognized

[3] Appeared in the *Southwestern Presbyterian*, March 18, 1869.

as a formal principle, approved by the reason and the conscience.

It is, moreover, an amiable theory—takes such gentle views of the laws of God—tones down the severity of that justice before which sin is ever trembling—and is so considerate of the vices of the heathen world, that your good people of exquisite sensibility glow with rapture over its discovery. It is, indeed, an appalling thought, that millions of the human race should be posting to the chambers of eternal death; and there are few, perhaps, who do not, at times, recoil from it, seeking some escape from the stern logic which compels its admission. Is not the divine Being infinite in mercy, and shall we presumptuously shut up every channel but one to its outflow? Must not justice discriminate between those who have 'sinned without law,' and those who have 'sinned in the law?' Shall those perish forever who have never so much as heard of the great remedy for sin which the gospel reveals to us? Such are some of the generalities into which men retreat from the pressure of the terrible conviction that without the knowledge of the Scriptures the Gentiles are irretrievably lost—a conviction which not only shocks the sensibilities, but disturbs the ease of the slothful. We need not expand the thought. It is easy to see how this fatal skepticism will paralyze all exertion; and how comfortably it nestles in the indolence which seeks exemption from toil, and in the sentimentalism which luxuriates in the pleasing and the soft.

But is it true? Reader, pause upon this question— the answer is pregnant with immortal destinies. If the heathen are independent of the gospel, and may find another road to heaven, it is the refinement of cruelty to proclaim it to them. It is better to exclude every ray of light from breaking in upon the blessed darkness which wraps them in such happy security; these are the consequences, on the one side of this momentous question. But if, on the other, it should be a mistake; alas, how awful! Countless millions, lifting up their voices eternally, to chide the guilty blunder which deliberately closed against them the gates of paradise! The presentation of the alternative seems to us to render all discussion impertinent. We only claim that it shall make the reader solemn in this attention to the argument.

1. In the very front then, we place the reply that *such a position discredits and impeaches the wisdom and goodness of God in providing a Savior at all.* The pen trembles under the blasphemy of the bare suggestion, which probes the objection to its core and exposes its absurdity. We know that the gift of a Savior is the fruit of infinite love. 'God so loved the world that he gave his only begotten Son, that whosoever believeth in him should not perish, but have everlasting life.' Who does not perceive that the very pivot on which this proof turns, is the implied impossibility of salvation to any without the gift of this Son? But if the heathen may be saved, simply through ignorance of the gospel, how much better it would have been to have had no gospel at all. Then all would stand upon the same footing, taking the equal chance of escaping through the meshes of the law which we have alike broken; and all would be free from the responsibility of rejecting

a Savior who was never given, to aggravate the doom
which impenitence and unbelief are sure to bring upon
the finally lost. This reasoning is not entirely our own.
Paul seems to have anticipated it when he says: 'If there
had been a law given which could have given life, verily,
righteousness should have been by the law; but the Scripture hath concluded all under sin, that the promise by
faith of Jesus Christ might be given to them that believe.'
The dilemma then is plainly this: either a divine Savior is
needed by all—in which case the heathen are as dependent upon the gospel as ourselves—or else, a Savior not
being required by any, the Christian world has occasion
to mourn over the light it enjoys, as sealing their eternal
doom. The death of Jesus Christ, so far from proving to
us the divine love, was the saddest of all mistakes. The
angel, instead of proclaiming at his birth, 'I bring you
good tidings of great joy which shall be to all people,'
did, in reality, chant the funeral dirge of a lost world, as
he thus canceled its last hope of life. The apostles, who
went everywhere preaching the Word, were the worst
enemies of the human race; and we, so far from sending
evangelists abroad, had better destroy this evangel ourselves, and subside at once, by a happy forfeiture of all
knowledge, into pagan darkness and security.

It is horrible to write all this. Yes, reader, and it is
horrible for you to think it—to have even the dark
suspicion lurking in the recesses of your mind. It is
infinitely better, because more truthful and manly, to
drag it forth to the light; to translate it into those very
horrible words, that you may look at both sides of the

dreadful alternative, and know which of the two makes you shudder the most. If you cannot bear to think of myriads of heathens lost forever, because they have *not* the gospel, can you bear to think of countless myriads sinking into still deeper perdition, because they *have* the gospel! Can you bear to think that when the divine compassion yearned over our apostate race, infinite wisdom should devise only a stupendous blunder, and infinite love should turn out the refinement of cruelty? If feeling and sentiment are to be judged in this case, they will find cause to be staggered in a decision which impeaches at once the wisdom, love and mercy of God in providing a Savior for lost man.

2. The assumption that the heathen can be saved without the gospel *is disproved by their actual moral condition in all periods of history.* The classic reader need not be reminded of the testimony of Persius and Juvenal, of Seneca, Tacitus and Pliny, showing the dark picture of heathen morality, drawn by the Apostle Paul, to be in no degree overwrought. And the reports of modern explorers and tourists reveal the fact that the somber coloring has not faded in the lapse of nineteen centuries. We will not repeat the dreadful details, which anyone may read for himself in the first chapter of Romans. But what shall a God of infinite purity do at last with those upon whom these hideous blotches are found? And how shall the Lawgiver dispense with the penalty which says: 'the soul that sinneth, it shall die'?

It is well, just here, to meet the fallacy upon which the whole theory is founded, which we are now discussing.

It is, throughout, assumed by these sentimentalists, that the heathen will be condemned, simply because they have not embraced a Savior, of whom they never heard; and, further, that in the final judgment no discrimination will be made between them and sinners who have rejected the gospel. Either assumption is unfounded. In reference to both, Paul's statement is explicit: 'As many as have sinned *without law*, shall also perish *without law*; and as many as have sinned *in the law*, shall be judged *by the law.*' These two classes are placed, each under its own dispensation. But, mark! Paul does not say that those who have sinned without law shall escape, and find a broad road to heaven through the divine compassion; but his fearful language is: they 'shall PERISH without law.' And in the following verse he expounds the principle on which the judgment, in their case, will proceed: 'For when the Gentiles—which have not the law—do by nature the things contained in the law, these, having not the law, are a law unto themselves, which show the work of the law written in their hearts; their consciences also bearing witness,' etc. (*Rom.* 2:12, 15). The heathen, then, who transgress the law of God written in their hearts, will be condemned for that transgression, and in precise accordance with the light and knowledge which they enjoy. The ground of condemnation will not be that they are without the gospel, but that they have violated that law to which their conscience bore witness; and the absence of the gospel has to do with their condemnation only so far that they are not saved from it through the gracious remedy which it provides.

But the sinner in Christian lands, who dies impenitent, will be condemned, not only for his breach of the law, but also for his rejection of the Savior; and will thus perish under an aggravated doom.

3. *We have the sure testimony of the Scriptures,* whose authority is final in a discussion like this. And this testimony might be presented under various classifications. For example: those passages may be recited which directly affirm the dependence of all men upon the gospel for salvation. Take but one instance out of many: 'There is no difference between the Jew and the Greek, for the same Lord is rich unto all that call upon him. For whosoever shall call upon the name of the Lord shall be saved. How, then, shall they call on him in whom they have not believed? And how shall they believe in him of whom they have not heard? And how shall they hear without a preacher?' Equally decisive is the whole passage in the first chapter of Romans, from the eighteenth verse to the end. Or we might group together those grand predictions of the world's evangelization, which, like the beautiful rainbow, span the whole arch of the Bible, from the first promise in Genesis to the splendid visions in the Apocalypse of John. Or, we might eliminate this testimony, as it pervades the whole texture of Bible thought—involved in all its doctrines of justification by faith, and the impossibility of salvation by works of the law. The result will be that every doctrine and every promise, every warning and every prophecy, will become a pointed testimony to the fact that without the cross of Jesus Christ the heathen are without hope forever.

4. It may be true that the gospel, if preached to the heathen, will be rejected by many, whose guilt will thus be proportionally increased. But all this is true at home as well as abroad; and constitutes as good a reason for the suppression here, as well as there. This is, however, a very inadequate view of the matter. The gospel, wherever it goes, finds out the Lord's hidden ones, 'the remnant according to the election of grace.' Its presence, anywhere on the globe, is evidence that some are there who shall be saved through its agency. It is an infinite gain to rescue these, whether they be many or whether they be few, from the general wreck. Since all have broken the law, and are swept away by that deluge of wrath which 'is revealed from heaven against all ungodliness and unrighteousness of men,' it is an infinite joy to rescue the few to whom the gospel proves 'the power of God to salvation.' Whilst looking, on the one side, to those to whom it proves 'the savor of death unto death,' let us not fail to regard those on the other, to whom it is 'the savor of life unto life.'

17

Thoughts upon
Foreign Missions—No. 4 [4]

NEWSPAPERS, above all periodicals, demand variety. For this reason, perhaps, a series of articles upon one subject proves tedious, even when the topic is of admitted importance. Prudence, therefore, dictates that this discussion should not be protracted beyond the present number. The reader will, however, be generous enough to allow the threads, spun in preceding papers, to be woven in something like a web, in this.

Three principal objections against the work of foreign missions have been considered. First—That the enterprise is chimerical. Second—That the church has enough to do at home. Third—That the heathen stand an even chance with ourselves to be saved, without the gospel.

[4] Appeared in the *Southwestern Presbyterian,* March 25, 1869.

Avoiding, then, the repetition of what has been already written, upon what general grounds may this great and solemn duty be enforced?

1st. We answer, *upon the plain command of Christ, himself.* Not to accumulate testimony, take the broad commission of the church: 'Go ye, therefore, and teach all nations; and lo! I am with you always, even to the end of the world.' What can be more explicit than this? And the solemn occasion on which it is uttered makes it as imperative as it is clear. The great redemption has been accomplished, and just when the Lord is about to ascend to his mediatorial throne, he gathers his little flock around him, and in the very act of parting, binds upon them this command, and enforces it with this peculiar promise. It is, henceforth, the charter upon which the church claims all her privileges—the broad commission upon which she fulfills her important functions. The sole warrant upon which she preaches the gospel to *one* single human being, is the command to preach it to *every* human being upon the face of the earth. Who will dare to cancel this injunction, and thus to seal the lips of this witness for the truth? And is there less presumption in the attempt to narrow the command, and to describe the parallels of latitude beyond which the voice of the herald shall not be heard?

In connection with this, the miraculous gift of tongues on the day of Pentecost was immensely significant. It indicated that this gospel should be proclaimed in all the languages into which the unity of human speech had been broken. When Parthians and

Medes, and Elamites, Cretes and Arabians, exclaimed in the streets of Jerusalem, 'We do hear them speak in our tongues the wonderful works of God!' this was, itself, a grand prophecy of the gospel's final triumph, when 'all the kingdoms of this world should become the kingdoms of our Lord and of his Christ.' By a symbol the most expressive, the Savior renewed his commission first given on the Mount of Olives, saying, again: 'Go ye into all the world and preach the gospel to every creature.' To us it is most impressive, that in the first exercise of his royal power, by which our Lord furnished evidence of his exaltation as a Prince and a Savior, he should also symbolize the church's work, and pledge her triumphant success.

2nd. Closely allied with the above, so as scarcely to be logically distinct, is *the idea of the gospel as a trust*. If the Bible be a revelation from heaven, it is, by virtue of that fact, the inheritance of mankind. If the death of Christ be an atonement for human guilt, we may no more monopolize it than the light we see, or the air we breathe. In the absence of any explicit directions, we might infer from the nature of these blessings, that we hold them under a strict requisition to give freely what we have freely received. Every Christian must exclaim with Paul, 'the glorious gospel of the blessed God, *which is committed to my trust!*'

Nay, it was the peculiar distinction of the Hebrew church that 'unto them were committed the oracles of God.' Stationary as that church was, anchored by her very ritual to one land, yet her mission was to keep the light of divine knowledge burning brightly upon her altars, that its rays might pierce the surrounding darkness, and woo the nations within her pale. And it is an instructive fact that, when faithless to her sacred trust at home, she is cast forth, a weeping exile, to bear witness for Jehovah 'by the rivers of Babylon.' For whilst that dismal captivity was visited upon them as a punishment for sin, it was none the less a providential arrangement by which the heathen world was prepared for the advent of Christ. If stationary Judaism was thus transformed, against its will, into a missionary agency, how much more must the Christian church go forth upon her grand itinerancy—the trustee for the nations of this great salvation?

3rd. Springing from the bosom of this thought is another, that *the heathen are sharers with us in the common ruin of the Fall.* Even a pagan could say, 'I think nothing human foreign from myself.' The 'one blood,' of which God hath made all nations, is felt to be the bond of universal brotherhood. We are united by common toil and grief in a fraternity of sorrow. The instincts and passions which throb in every human breast are recognized as the badges of a common nature, which it is unlawful to disown. Upon this principle, the tie of common guilt binds us to the heathen, with the strongest obligation. Equally related with ourselves to that 'first disobedience' which 'brought death into the world, and all our woe,' they are partners with us in this dismal inheritance. They lie, equally crushed, beneath the ruins of the first covenant; and to be insensible to their wretchedness, is to violate the law of humanity with most atrocious cruelty. The solemnity of the thought lies in the crime we commit against *ourselves* in bursting the bonds of human brotherhood, and trampling upon the purest impulses of human sympathy.

4th. *This duty is doctrinally involved in our living union with Christ, our Head.* We do not speak here of the love and gratitude which we owe to the Savior, as an external benefactor. All this is very true, and it has often been addressed pungently to the Christian conscience. But it is too general and vague for the purpose we now have in hand. We mean to say that Christians, as the members of Christ, are led by this living union of their Head, to undertake and to accomplish all the work that is dear to his heart. Nor can we draw back from it without feeling the strain put upon all the cords that bind us to him. Is Christ *the Prophet* that should come into the world, so that 'No man knoweth the Father, save he to whomsoever the Son will reveal him?' Then are we, too, the Lord's prophets, to bear the words of his revelation around the globe. He, the Prophet, now in his person withdrawn, discharges his office by the agency of those whom he has brought into union with himself. Hence, at the ascension 'He gave some, apostles; and some, prophets; and some, evangelists; and some, pastors and teachers.' 'The Lord gave the Word; great was the company of those who published it.' Is Christ a Priest? Then are we in him 'a royal priesthood,' to bear his own great atoning sacrifice, and lay it before the heathen, in the room of their bulls and goats, which can never take away sin. Is Christ a King? Then hath he appointed us as kings with himself; that, sharing in the toil of conquest, we may share in his final victory, and sit down with him upon his throne.

Let us reproduce the thought in a more particular and concrete form. The Father saith to the Son, 'Ask of me, and I will give thee the heathen for thine inheritance, and the uttermost parts of the earth for thy possession.' Now, how does the Redeemer comply with this condition, and in what way does he ask of the Father? Undoubtedly by his simple presence in heaven, where he points to the stipulations of the covenant, and authoritatively claims his own. But, undoubtedly, also, by sealing his own petition upon the lips of his own believing people, and by teaching them to pray to this Father, 'Thy kingdom come; thy will be done on earth, as it is done in heaven!' Sweet and tender thought! That in all our toils, and alms, and prayers, it is the Christ in us who longs to 'see of the travail of his soul, and be satisfied!' And those supernatural gifts with which the apostolic church was for a time endowed, have they not their chief significance in showing the close connection between the church on earth and the great Head in heaven?—the pledge, too, to her, that all needed help should be hers, to the end of time, by which to fulfill her holy mission.

5th. *The church can never desert the brave hearts* which have given themselves to this blessed work. There will be those who rise above the skepticism and apathy of their times, who will see the pathetic gestures of their

Lord pointing to those, stumbling upon the dark mountains of idolatry, and saying, 'Other sheep I have, which
are not of this fold'; and who will feel that, for Christ's
sake, they are 'debtors, both to the Greeks and to the
barbarians.' Can we sit down in our pleasant places,
withholding sympathy and succor from our own representatives, who sacrifice country and home, and even
life itself, to fulfill the duty which is common to us and
them? All that is generous and true in the sanctified
heart utters a protest against selfishness so base and cruel.

In our own church God has put the signal mark of
his approval, within the year past, by raising up in the
midst of her sons, a small but noble band of evangelists,
who say, 'Here are we—send us.'

But a short time since we saw ourselves cut off from
the sympathies of Christendom, with our old ministry
dying out, and no quarter from which its ranks could be
recuperated. We spread forth our hands to him whom
we worship and obey as our Master and Head; and lo!
there springs up, all over the church, a large class of
candidates, who are now under training, for the gospel
ministry. And now, co-ordinate with this, seven or
eight young missionaries have seized the banner of the
church, and planted it on heathen soil. What does God
say in all this? 'I will repair your wastes—and give you
the men to go into the harvest; with this seal of my
blessing I summon you to the great work for which the
church was instituted; and I give you the men who shall
inaugurate that work, and so pledge you to its execu-
tion.' Such seems to us to be the plain interpretation

of God's providence to our Southern Church. Let the response from us be a solemn pledge to uphold, with sympathy and constant aid, all who go from our bosom to bring the nations unto God.[5]

[5] Palmer is referring to the bedraggled Presbyterian Church in the United States, which had its origins from 1861. Ostracized from its mother church (the Presbyterian Church in the United States of America, commonly called The Northern Church after 1861) and other like-faith communions, and decimated by war and Reconstruction, the PCUS (commonly called the Southern Church) began to establish a Foreign Mission enterprise as early as 1866. For a brief discussion see C. N. Willborn, 'Southern Presbyterianism: The Character of a Tradition,' in *Confessing Our Hope,* Joseph Pipa and C. N. Willborn, ed. (Taylors, SC: Southern Presbyterian Press, 2004), especially pp. 303-10.

18

The Unknown Way[6]

'I will bring the blind by a way they know not'
(*Isa.* 42:16)

PERHAPS no sinner was ever brought to Christ
in the way he expected. We preconceive a certain
method of conversion and dwell upon it so fondly, as to
come at last to think it cannot take place otherwise. We
fancy that it is indispensable to pass through exceedingly

[6] Appeared in the *Southwestern Presbyterian*, March 10, 1870.
While this article does not follow the preceding 'Foreign Missions'
articles chronologically, it follows logically for it sets forth the biblical emphasis upon the sovereignty of God in saving sinners. Focus
upon God's sovereignty drives practitioners of Christianity to the
simple means of grace prescribed in the Holy Scriptures. It drives
the church to the preaching of the gospel as the *sine qua non* and
primus of the gospel mission. In our age the gospel has been com-
promised and often lost as the means of evangelizing the masses
and converting the soul. Thus, we include this article as a hope-
ful encouragement to those tired of culture-based, gimmick-filled
methods of evangelism and missions.—*Editor.*

pungent convictions rising even into anguish which will then suddenly yield to a brilliant and overpowering sense of forgiveness and acceptance with God. Our reason teaches that we ought to have just these distressing views of sin, as infinitely hateful in itself, and so we conclude that we must necessarily have them. Such an experience too appears to be so satisfactory, by reason of the strong contrasts which it presents, that we begin to feel as if no other evidence would satisfy us that we have really passed from death to life.

How often, on the contrary, does the sinner find all his efforts vain, in lashing himself up to this pitch of agony! He turns the sharp points of the law in upon his own conscience, and lacerates himself with its fierce accusations: yet in spite of all, his feelings will not flow in the prescribed channel. God chooses to subdue him by a process entirely different. He is only conscious of a stronger fascination, by which he is held to the subject of religion so that he cannot slide into indifference; until, in a way perfectly unaccountable, his opposition to God crumbles to dust, and he discovers himself falling into the arms of divine mercy. Or else, the love, which the gospel breathes, steals insensibly over his spirit; and he is gently moved, without the consuming terrors of the law, to the Savior's embrace.

There would be no particular harm in these mistaken preconceptions of the way by which he is to be led, if they did not seriously embarrass his recognition of the work of grace, when it is actually wrought. The great change has occurred in a manner so unexpected, that he cannot for a time accept it as real. He has first to learn that there is more than one door to the human soul, and that the free Spirit of God has the keys of them all, and can enter by whichsoever of them he pleases. Until this is understood, all his evidences of grace are clouded: simply because he will insist upon one form of experience, and will recognize no other.

There are good reasons, however, why the Lord should disappoint these anticipations, and lead the sinner by a way he knew not. For example: it might be exceedingly perilous, in many cases, to indulge him in the preference which he avows. The simple fact that he clings with such tenacity to this antecedent anguish as indispensable to true peace, shows that he exaggerates its value. It is so easy to glide into the notion that this is a set-off to the account betwixt himself and God. There is a hidden complacency in the reflection, that if he has been a great sinner, he has had at least the decency to feel very badly about it. The mere assumption of a moral sensibility, which has occasioned so much suffering, ministers to his self-love, strengthens the natural ligations of the heart, and forestalls the deep humility which God so much approves. Divine wisdom therefore shields him from this great peril, by bringing him to the cross in such a way that he can find nothing in himself of which to boast. The very fact too that the sinner recognizes this predetermined experience as so peculiarly satisfactory, makes it dangerous that he will trust to it, instead of leaning wholly upon Christ. Just because he can detect these amazing contrasts between now and then, he is exposed to the fearful hazard of making a savior out of his own fancies, to the disparagement of him who has bought us with his own blood.

It must be remembered also that God guards, with a most sacred jealousy, his own prerogatives of sovereignty. It is this attribute against which we are the most likely to impinge in the natural operation of our own personality. It is this very perfection which was openly discredited in the first transgression; requiring it to be the more conspicuously indicated in this sphere of grace. By just so much as the divine Being binds himself by covenant pledges, must he at the same time illustrate the majesty and supremacy of his law. While therefore he fulfills to the penitent soul every promise of his gracious Word, he leads into his own peace by methods which are determined by his own pleasure, and not by those which our caprices would dictate. Every Christian is made to understand this, more and more perfectly, in the marvelous ways by which God answers his pious prayers, and through the strange delays so often interposed in his providence. How important that it should form the initial lesson, taught the neophyte as he passes into the kingdom of grace!

Nor is it consistent with the riches of the divine wisdom and love, that there should be a stereotyped and uniform procedure in bringing men to salvation. While the elements of Christian experience are the same, their combination is varied almost endlessly: and the circumstances under which character is developed, are as diverse as the providence of God can make them. It is not a little instructive, that, side by side, in the same chapter, should be given the history of the jailer, brought to the Savior amid the terrors of the earthquake, and the conversion of Lydia whose heart the Lord opened to hear the words that were spoken of Paul. Thus, by diversity in his methods, does it please God to illustrate the wealth of his resources: even in bestowing the same blessing upon each, of eternal life.

This conclusion of the whole is, that God's way of bringing the sinners to the light, is the best way. It is the best because it is *his* way: the safest to the believer, because guarded against dangers which he scarcely suspects; and the happiest, because furnished with the freest tokens of the divine favor. Instead therefore of choosing his own path, let the awakened sinner surrender himself entirely to the Spirit's guidance, who will lead him along gently and without the possibility of fatal mistake.

PART THREE

The Beatitudes

Blessed are the poor in spirit: for theirs is the kingdom of heaven. Blessed are they that mourn: for they shall be comforted. Blessed are the meek: for they shall inherit the earth. Blessed are they which do hunger and thirst after righteousness: for they shall be filled. Blessed are the merciful: for they shall obtain mercy. Blessed are the pure in heart: for they shall see God. Blessed are the peacemakers: for they shall be called the children of God. Blessed are they which are persecuted for righteousness' sake: for theirs is the kingdom of heaven. Blessed are ye, when men shall revile you, and persecute you, and shall say all manner of evil against you falsely, for my sake. Rejoice, and be exceeding glad: for great is your reward in heaven: for so persecuted they the prophets which were before you.

Matthew 5:3-12

19

The Seven Beatitudes[1]

THE exposition of these Beatitudes, in the Commentaries to which the ordinary reader has access, is to the last degree, unsatisfactory. The capital defect seems to consist in regarding them in the light of *ethical* propositions, simply. Under this view it is difficult to trace any logical distinction between them, so that they may be kept apart without returning upon each other. For example: 'the poor in spirit,' in the first, 'the meek,' in the third, and 'the merciful,' in the fifth, shade so insensibly into one another, when viewed only as moral apothegms, that an interpreter finds himself blending their lights, and sliding into the vaguest generalities, in order to make even a show of explanation that shall not be darker than the text.

But what increases the reader's dissatisfaction is the utter barrenness of the results yielded. He instinctively

---

[1] Appeared in the *Southwestern Presbyterian,* January 6, 1870.

feels them to be immeasurably short of what might be expected in 'the Sermon on the Mount.' The greatest of all teachers, in the very opening of his ministry, cannot be supposed to employ such a magnificent exordium, unless it has a deeper meaning than so jejune an exposition affords. The heart will be satisfied with nothing less than the *gospel* in these splendid sentences. They must be *evangelical*, or they are not in tone with the discourse which they introduce. The key to this wonderful sermon is found in Matthew 3:2, and 4:17. John the Baptist—the forerunner—had announced the kingdom of the Messiah as at hand. Christ commences his own ministry with the same proclamation. At a later period the seventy are sent forth with the same announcement. Of course, the inquiry would arise: what is the nature of this kingdom? what the law under which it is administered? what the character of its subjects? and what its relation to the old dispensation under Moses? To these, and similar questions, the Sermon on the Mount gives determinative answers; not in the way of scientific theological discussion, nor yet in the way of cold ethical propositions, but as an easy and simple exposition of the nature of the gospel. Hence, it opens with the voice of blessing; and these seven benedictions afford a true delineation of the Christian character, and of the successive stages by which the Christian life is accomplished.

This presents the clue to a clear and satisfactory exposition. We have the whole gospel of our blessed Lord, sketched in profile, and all the elements of a true Christian experience—as they are—progressively unfolded under the agency and influence of the Holy Ghost. Lange says: 'In the succession of these beatitudes, Christ marks the development of the new life, from its commencement to its completion.' And Stier says: 'Such are the seven benedictions, which embrace the Christian discipleship: the regeneration, in its development from poverty of spirit, into all that is contained in the true and essential filial relation to God.'

In the present paper we shall content ourselves with a general analysis. According to Stier, whose view we approve above all others, these beatitudes break into two sections. The first *three* describe the process by which a sinner is brought to God: 'the poor in spirit' are those who are made to feel their emptiness, and need—this deepens, in the second, into a true sense of sin, and into godly mourning for it, and this, in turn, into the third, to that breaking down of the proud will, when, as 'the meek,' it is ready to receive the salvation of God. In the fourth, the believing soul accepts Christ as all its righteousness, and is accepted in the Beloved. This, being the point of transition, connects the first three with the last three benedictions—which series exhibits the development of the new life now begun in the Christian. In 'the merciful,' a holy love shows itself in acts of mercy and kindness to others; in 'the pure in heart,' we have the whole work of sanctification, as carried on *within* the soul; in 'the peacemakers,' we have represented the whole activity of the Christian life, as it seeks to evangelize the world. In this work of reconciling a lost race to God, it meets with conflict and persecution, out of which springs a supplemental benediction, which is the climax of the whole.

The construction is strikingly similar to that of the Lord's prayer, which, in like manner, divides into two classes of petition: the first, embracing the superior relations in which we stand to God; the second, the lower earthly relations which we also sustain. Exactly, too, as the fourth petition mediates between those pairs, so the fourth benediction forms the link between the two pairs into which the beatitudes are divided. The same arrangement obtains in the Decalogue, where the fifth commandment forms, through the parental relation, the transition from the first to the second table of the law.

20

The Poor in Spirit[2]

PERHAPS the best explanation of this expression is found in Revelation 3:17—'because those sayest I am rich and increased in goods, and have need of nothing; and knowest not that thou art wretched and miserable, and poor, and blind, and naked.' This language exactly describes the condition of the sinner in his estrangement from God. Puffed up with the conceit of his own wisdom and goodness, and a deceived heart turning him aside to the world as the source of enjoyment, he wraps himself in the mantle of complacency, and says that he 'has need of nothing.' The first step, therefore, in his salvation, is when the Holy Spirit strips off this disguise, and reveals to him his utter emptiness and need. It is here that this work of conviction ordinarily begins; and the phrase, 'poor in spirit,' covers that earliest and most bitter experience, when the sinner first knows that he is 'poor and

---

[2] Appeared in the *Southwestern Presbyterian,* January 13, 1870.

miserable, and blind, and naked.' In the general outline of these beatitudes, given last week, we construed the first three as distinguishing that stage which we generically call 'conviction for sin,' and through which the awakened soul passes to faith in Christ, and to acceptance with God. This beatitude, then, as the first of the series, expresses the initial germ of this conviction, in a sense of spiritual bankruptcy and ruin.

We do not mean to intimate that this feeling of emptiness and want exists by itself, and alone, as separated from the 'mourning' and the 'nakedness' which are afterwards described. On the contrary, all our kindred emotions shade, insensibly, into each other, and blend into our common habit, or frame of the soul, just as the colors of the spectrum blend in the white light which is the product of them all. But we do not hesitate to regard the violet, red and indigo as distinct rays, simply because the eye cannot distinguish where the one ends and other begins. It is their real distinction, together with this interpenetration, which produces the common and joint effect. Precisely so we are obliged, in our logical analysis, to take up this or that feeling, and view it apart, however we may find it coordinated with other feelings in actual experience. Undoubtedly, when the sinner is turned from darkness to light, there is a beginning of the process, somewhere; and that initial feeling we may consider by itself, however soon it may intermingle with others in a complex experience. In the science of mathematics we think of a point before we think of a line, although the point may instantly lose itself in the line which it generates.

It is not unsafe to say that the beginning point in every case of true conversion is the feeling of dissatisfaction with self, and with the world. Satiety overtakes us at the height of earthly enjoyment, and we turn, in quick succession, from one pursuit to another, crying, as we change, 'who will show us any good?' The moment is critical. We are either drawn towards God, from whose fullness our immortal longings shall be satisfied; or we turn back to the 'weak and beggarly elements,' and harness ourselves to the world as its servant and drudge. So, too, the Holy Spirit takes off the veil from our own hearts, and self-complacency gives way to shame, under the discovery of our own vileness and sin. We turn, upon this disclosure, as upon a pivot, either to the Great Physician, and are healed, or else we debauch the conscience, and live contented with our own degradation. In these benedictions, however, our Lord is disclosing the spiritual nature of his kingdom; and, of course, the first will express that sense of emptiness and want in which renewing grace commences the work of a sound conversion. This 'poverty of spirit' is, therefore, to be taken in its widest scope, extending from that earliest feeling of displacency and unrest in the sinner's heart, to the permanent humility and sense of dependence in which the Christian goes out of himself, and finds all his resources in God.

Of such, then, Jesus adds, 'theirs is the kingdom of heaven.' The reader does not require to be told that this phrase is employed in Scripture in a threefold sense. Sometimes it refers to the blessedness and joys of heaven;

sometimes, to the state of grace, into which the believer is introduced by the new birth; sometimes, to the organized and visible church of the Redeemer, on the earth. All these significations are, however, closely related. The word runs along upon the line of *grace*; as it is begun in the Christian's individual experience at conversion—as it is developed through the discipline and training of the visible church, into which all true believers are supposed to be articulated; and, finally, as this grace is consummated in the glory of the eternal state. A perfect unity of sentiment thus underlies the three senses of this word: there is the same substantive holiness in each, in different stages of development; the same employment in each—obedience and worship; the same enjoyments in them all, a foretaste of heaven being provided for the Christian, while here upon earth.

This first beatitude, therefore, is both declarative and promissory. It sets forth the nature of a gracious state, and the qualifications of membership in the church militant, as beginning in true 'poverty of spirit.' All pride and self-sufficiency are to be renounced by those who find grace and eternal life in the Savior; and to all such as are the true subjects of his spiritual kingdom here below, he promises the final rewards which are reserved for them in heaven.

21

Blessed Are They That Mourn[3]

THE first beatitude we have seen to express that sense of want, which, as in the case of the prodigal son, in the Lord's parable, is the point of the sinner's arrest in his guilty wandering from God. Beginning, however, only in this, we have construed it only as a spiritual grace—stretching on through the whole experience of the Christian, in the constant out-going from himself, to the infinite sufficiency of the Creator.

This 'poverty of spirit' deepens, now, in the second beatitude, into a gracious 'mourning' for sin, which covers the whole doctrine of repentance. It is a far deeper sentiment than the other. Then, the sinner found himself 'poor and miserable, and blind and naked;' now, he traces this wretchedness to its source, in his own guilt and sin. We recognize in it the law-work of the spirit, in conviction for sin; as sketched in the apostle's words:

[3] Appeared in the *Southwestern Presbyterian,* January 20, 1870.

'I was alive without the law once; but when the commandment came, sin revived, and I died.'

The word 'mourn' is chosen by our Lord to describe exactly the nature of the emotion. It is, first of all, the feeling of bereavement, which steals over the heart when first it discovers its condition of orphanage, 'without God in the world'! This may mount through various degrees of distress: now rising into the poignancy of anguish, and now existing in the force of permanent uneasiness and unrest. The stress is not laid here, but upon the quality of the emotion, which the Savior marks as the melancholy sense of loneliness and loss. The soul mourns after the God whose presence it craves; and the sadness of bereavement can only be removed by a sense of perfect reconciliation.

In the next place, there is a clear discovery of the true nature of sin, as displeasing to that great Being, whose society and love are now so intensely desired. The apostle hence distinguishes between 'the godly' and 'the worldly' sorrow, in true repentance. The latter contemplates sin in its consequences, which are dreadful enough; the former regards it in its essential nature, which is more dreadful still. The one beholds it in the light of the divine justice; the other in the contrast of the divine purity. It is not, as the moralist supposes, simply the mortification of falling below our own ideal of excellence—for this is often the most sullen manifestation of pride. But it is just that melancholy into which a true heart saddens, when it discovers the infinite contradiction in sin to all that is lovely and glorious in God.

So that, here, again, the word delineates the character of the sentiment, which, more than its degree, is the important thing to be noticed.

Then, in the third place, this sin is perceived, not in the abstract, but as cleaving to ourselves. Thus the soul comes to feel its taint, as well as its curse. It is not simply the guilt, but the defilement of it which fills the penitent with grief. It is not only fear, indulged in view of the penalty, but a hearty loathing of the fatal leprosy, which is felt to be as rottenness in the bones. It takes up all actual transgressions, and ascends to the sin, of the nature itself of which they are but the diagnosis. But the predominant character of the emotion is signalized in the Savior's word for it: it is grief; all the pathos of the profoundest melancholy lodges in the phrase; 'they that *mourn.*'

And now the reader sees with what consistency and reach of meaning the word is carried over to all the afflictions of this sorrowful life. All sorrow is derived through sin. Even when visited in gracious discipline, it is God's testimony against transgression—always most emphatic when visited upon those whom he most conspicuously loves. This it is that gives such peculiar edge to the afflictions of life, when the sensibility is awakened to trace the subtle connection. 'The sting of death is sin;' and what is death but the comprehension of all the evils which man suffers here below? Thus does this well-selected word of the Great Teacher sweep over the entire gamut of the Christian's experience, beginning with the earliest contrition of the heart for discovered sin, and embracing all those sorrows which darken life until they are swallowed in the deeper gloom of the grave.

Yet shall these be 'comforted.' And the loving Master can fall upon no other word for expressing this, but that word which he employs in John's Gospel, to designate 'the Paraclete,' whom he should send after his departure. 'They shall be comforted!' yes, by being *called up* out of their sin and sorrow, *alongside* of him who is their portion and their joy! Thus the word runs along through all the stages of ripening grace. They are 'comforted:'

First, by the call of the gospel, itself, to repose on the Savior; touching, at the outset, that mystery of human experience, where hope is seen to spring from the very bosom of despair—in which the naked principle of hope is sustained by simply looking at the provisions of mercy, and before the sense of acceptance with God begins to dawn upon the soul. Then,

Secondly, by the sealing of pardon upon the conscience, which is at once discharged of its burden, and rejoices in the hope of the glory of God. Then,

Thirdly, by the perpetual opening of the promises of grace to our faith, in all the times of need, by which we gain strength to resist the tempter, and rise out of fear into a free and joyful assurance. Then,

Fourthly, by the consciousness of actual deliverance from the dominion and power of sin, in our advancing sanctification, as we draw nearer the eternal rest. Then,

Fifthly, by the sweet sense of personal communion with the Father, and with his Son, Jesus Christ, in which are showered upon us the tokens of the divine favor. And,

Finally, we are 'comforted' with all the blessedness of heaven, of which our spiritual joys, here below, are the prophecy and pledge, and which, hereafter, is bestowed as the reward of grace—making full compensation for all the pain of that discipline by which we have been rendered meet for the inheritance of glory.

Thus, the nature of 'the mourning,' and of 'the solace,' is depicted in the well-chosen words of Christ.

22

Blessed Are the Meek[4]

THE ethical interpretation is utterly insipid which construes 'the meek' into the gentle and forbearing, simply, and evaporates the promise into the bold declaration that such enjoy, with more comfort than others, the portion which providence allots. If these opening sentences of our Lord's sermon are intended to vindicate the spirituality of true religion from the glosses of a merely traditional orthodoxy, then 'the meekness' of this beatitude must be viewed not only on its human side, as between man and man, but must express the deeper religious feeling towards God.

When the sense of emptiness and need, first awakened in the sinner's heart, has deepened into genuine sorrow for sin, we would logically expect the justification to follow, which is the subject of the fourth benediction. But, with most singular accuracy, the Great Teacher pauses for a moment, and, in the use of a single critical

[4] Appeared in the *Southwestern Presbyterian*, January 27, 1870.

136

word, marks that state of mind just antecedent to the actual reception of the Savior, viz.: that entire breaking down of the sinner's will, and the purely receptive frame necessary to an embrace of the gospel. Let us illustrate this point a little. Suppose a bankrupt incarcerated by a relentless creditor; he would feel himself utterly poor and miserable, and might reflect seriously upon his own want of forethought, if not upon actual recklessness and folly, and would earnestly pray for some kind hand of relief. Let one now enter his gloomy cell, and propose, not only to cancel the debt, but even to re-instate him in his former affluence, upon this sole condition—that it shall be accepted as a gratuity throughout, with no thought of repayment in the future. Is it not conceivable that a proud and self-reliant man would chafe at the humiliation of the proposal, and, while acutely sensible of his own wretchedness, that he might reject it altogether? The first impulse would probably be to decline an obligation so weighty; until, reflecting upon the kindness and generosity of the offer, obstinacy and pride begin gradually to yield, and the consent of the will is finally and fully gained. This fully represents the sinner's attitude towards the law, and towards the Savior. He owes a debt which he cannot pay. Under legal conviction, he feels his poverty and ruin, and mourns over the sin which occasions it. But when Christ comes and offers to him a free salvation, his pride and self-love remonstrate, until, melted down by the generosity of divine grace, he reaches the point of complete surrender to the gospel method of salvation.

This, then, is exactly what is expressed here by the word 'meek,' on the side which looks towards God, while the human side is that of gentleness and forbearance towards man. It is very worthy of our notice, in this connection, with what precision this word is used in the Scriptures to denote this attitude of submission to God's way of justifying the sinner. David says: 'the meek will he guide in judgment, and the meek will he teach his way.' Again, 'He will beautify the meek with salvation.' Isaiah declares that the Messiah was 'anointed to preach good tidings unto the meek;' and, as parallel with this, the Apostle James exhorts us to 'receive, with meekness, the engrafted word.' In all these passages it is assumed that the sinner must be brought into that submissive frame of soul denoted as meekness, before he can profit by the word of life, which is addressed to the conscience and heart.

The struggle, at which we have hinted, has a three-fold source, and must be passed through in every case, more or less severe, until the same result is reached in all. It springs,

1. *From the consciousness of our own personality.* Each man is a person, with an individual will which he must habitually exercise. We are prone to assert this against God, in the same manner as against our fellow-men, until, through the Holy Spirit, we learn to exercise it in the way of submission; not merging our personality, which is an impossibility, but consciously subordinating it, just as the wife and child freely exercise their wills in submission.

2. *Our relations to God being originally those of the law, it is difficult to comprehend the idea of grace,* or the receiving of God's favor without an equivalent. This continues till we are divinely enlightened, and we see the actual glory of Christ's righteousness imputed to us.

3. *Sin so utterly estranges us from God, that nothing is more distasteful than this dependence upon grace.* Hence the heart must be renewed before the will can be brought into this state of acquiescence.

'The meek,' then, are those who, overwhelmed by the magnanimity of the gospel, and sweetly persuaded by the Holy Ghost, yield all resistance to the offer of free salvation, and are prepared instantly to accept Christ as their 'wisdom, righteousness, sanctification and redemption.' Developed from this beginning, the word represents that permanent spiritual grace which, in the Christian, continually repudiates self-righteousness, and 'counts all things but loss for the excellency of the knowledge of Christ Jesus the Lord.' It marks the anti-legal spirit which more and more finds salvation, not in the law, but in 'Christ, who is the end of the law for righteousness, to every one that believeth.'

The promise to such is, that '*they shall inherit the earth.*' This form of language is evidently carried over from the Old Testament; when God entered into covenant with Abraham, and gave to him and to his seed the land of Canaan, with all its typical significance, for an inheritance forever. (See *Gen.* 15:7, 18; *Gen.* 17:8; *Psa.* 25:13; *Psa.* 37:11, 22; *Isa.* 60:21). This gives a clue to its interpretation:

1. *That the righteous are in covenant with God.* Since the blessings are couched in that old covenant language with which Israel was already familiar; and which is an eternal covenant only as it is spiritually fulfilled to the true seed of Abraham.

2. *It implies, that whatever earthly portion the righteous enjoy, comes to them by inheritance as the children of God.* Other principles may determine how much that portion shall actually be; but the covenant secures all that is necessary, which is the sweeter for being an inheritance.

3. *It implies that the whole earth belongs to the righteous,* which they posses through their divine Head—to be realized as theirs in the glory of the millennium, and in the new heaven and new earth wherein righteousness shall dwell.

4. As the earthly inheritance is typical of the heavenly, this promise looks through the telescope of prophecy to *the final reward and blessedness of the eternal state.*

Such is 'the meekness' described by our Lord. Not natural pliancy, or easiness of disposition, but a spiritual grace, such as was wrought in the constitutionally irascible Moses, and the impatient Job, and in all those in whom Divine grace verifies its paradox, and who out of weakness are made strong.

23

Hungering and Thirsting
after Righteousness[5]

THE first three beatitudes trace the sinner's progress
from the earliest sense of his own poverty, through
sincere mourning for sin, to the breaking down of all
pride and self-will—when he is in the posture to receive
eternal life as the gift of grace. The fourth benediction
takes him just at this point, and presents him in the
exercise of that faith which 'receives Christ and rests
upon him alone for salvation.' The reference, therefore, is mainly to righteousness *imputed*; the word being
signalized, in the original, by the article, so as properly
to be rendered '*the* righteousness.' Inherent righteousness need not, however, be rigorously excluded; since all
the elements of true piety are grouped together in these
beatitudes, without being always sharply discriminated.
Under this view, the sentence covers the whole doctrine

[5] Appeared in the *Southwestern Presbyterian,* February 3, 1870.

of our justification before God; precisely as we shall hereafter find the sixth benediction covering the whole work of progressive sanctification.

The interpretation then touches, first, the import of the metaphor, '*hungering and thirsting* after righteousness.' It involves:

1. *A real sympathy with the righteousness of Christ, as commensurate with the holiness of the law.* No man has true conviction for sin, but through the law which perfectly reveals the divine holiness. It is the felt inadequacy of his own righteousness to meet the same, which drives the sinner to cry out for 'a days-man who shall lay his hand upon them both.' As soon as the Holy Spirit reveals to him the completeness of Christ's vicarious obedience, he chooses this and rejects his own. His sole desire is now 'to be found in Christ, not having his own righteousness which is of the law, but that which is through the faith of Christ, the righteousness which is of God by faith.' The process is precisely this in every case of sound conversion, however more or less clearly the several steps may be defined in our reflective consciousness. In every case there is a real sympathy with divine rectitude, and a hearty appreciation and embrace of Christ's righteousness as commensurate with it. This is the act of faith in our justification.

2. *This 'hungering' implies a perpetual recurrence to this righteousness of the Savior, as satisfying our need.* Hunger and thirst do not simply express a present desire; they are constant appetites, in the gratification of which the body is daily refreshed, and the regular recurrence of which is a

sign of vigorous health. In like manner, faith is not only an act, but a habit of the soul. It is a constant principle, eventuating in particular acts of trust; just as appetite in the body leads to the reception of food through which it is sustained. For his own comfort, the believer yearns for a righteousness which is perfect; and thus is driven out of himself to a new and continued appropriation of his blessed Lord and Head. His daily language is, 'the life that I now live in the flesh, I live by the faith of the Son of God, who loved me and gave himself for me.'

3. *Then, finally, there is the outworking of all this in our own personal obedience.* It is important to trace the connection, as well as the distinction, between righteousness *inherent* and *imputed.* The former is not the cause of justification, but the result and proof of it. The renewed soul will have none but a perfect righteousness, and so it takes that of Christ. But this, enshrined within, reflects through the whole character and life. The same sympathy with holiness which led to an honest appropriation of Christ's offered obedience, will equally manifest itself in the continual effort to reproduce it in acts of personal conformity with the law of God. It is the normal exhibition of the true spiritual life within. Thus the doctrine of free justification is vindicated from the charges of licentiousness: 'how shall we that are dead to sin, live any longer therein?'

The rich promise to such is, that *'they shall be filled.'* This is realized to the Christian:

1. *In the clear sense, that the righteousness of Christ is by faith made his own.* Evidently we could not be justified

through the obedience of another, so long as it remains exclusively his; and the essence of true faith is that power of appropriation by which we make it ours. In the act of faith there is the concurrent exercise of all the faculties of the soul; so that it brings into play the whole moral nature, and is a perfect test of our agency as reasonable beings. Just as our own obedience would be recognized as *ours*, because it is the product of our own agency; so the obedience of Christ is felt to be *ours*, because the whole complement of our faculties has gone into the faith which appropriates it. In this conversion of owner-ship—as complete as though the righteousness consisted in the matter of our own obedience to the law—the believer begins to be 'filled.'

2. *This promise is further redeemed in the conscious repose of the soul upon the satisfaction and work of the Redeemer.* This state of rest must follow, because the creature now leans upon his God in the fullest manifestation of his power and goodness. Sin, too, which wrought such dis-turbance is taken away forever; and righteousness is pos-sessed which satisfies both conscience and the law. The entire soul, in the harmonious action of all its powers, pours itself forth in the embrace of Christ, and is thus equally poised upon its center of rest.

3. *The believer is increasingly 'filled,' through a growing sense of the glory of this righteousness of his Lord.* The law, being the revelation of God's rectitude, must be forever immeasurable to the creature; and the obedience of Christ as an exhaustive satisfaction of its claims, must be equal in extent. Its glory will open, therefore, upon the

saint forever. In addition to this, every new discovery of sin, every new form of temptation, every new trial of grief, leads back to Christ and to new aspects of the glory of his work. With this enlargement of the Christian's experience, will there be an increased 'filling with this righteousness.'

4. *Co-ordinate with this, will be the advance in personal holiness*; making the imputed righteousness of Christ, on which it substantially rests, all the sweeter to the heart.

5. *The perfection of the promise will be enjoyed in heaven,* when Christ's glory will be fully seen, and the believer will find his right to a place among the heavenly hosts determined simply by his relation to his Head. 'The city had no need of the sun, neither of the moon to shine in it; for the glory of God did lighten it, and THE LAMB IS THE LIGHT THEREOF.'

24

Blessed Are the Merciful[6]

SCRIPTURE is always the best interpreter of Scripture; simply, because it all proceeds from one source,
and its various parts form an organic whole. The clue to
this fifth beatitude is furnished in the fifth petition of
the Lord's prayer; which is the only one expressly cou-
pled with a vow, 'forgive us our debts as we forgive our
debtors.' This, of course, does not imply that forgiveness on our part is the meritorious or procuring cause of
the forgiveness we experience from God. It simply sets
forth the obligation imposed on us to forgive, and is the
seal and pledge that we have been ourselves forgiven. So
when these beatitudes have traced the sinner's progress
to the moment of repentance and of faith, the question
arises, how will this reconciled believer now behave,
and what evidence will be furnished of a gracious state?
The answer is returned in the three last beatitudes,

[6] Appeared in the *Southwestern Presbyterian*, February 10, 1870.

which describe the whole career of the Christian. In his relations to men, he will show the mercy he has himself received; in his relations to God, he will strive after perfect holiness of heart; and being in full sympathy both with man and God, he will identify himself with the Peacemaker, in the great work of reconciling a lost world to God.

The exhibition of mercy will then always be a characteristic of the renewed soul.

1. *Because of the new faith in which he is recast in God's image, and made partaker of the divine nature.* God's mercy is only a manifestation of his essential goodness, viewing the creature as guilty and undeserving. The new nature, by its own law of life, must work itself out of the exhibitions of the perfections in God which are communicable; especially that love, which is so peculiarly divine.

2. *The Christian cannot but sympathize with the wretchedness of the race to which he belongs.* The necessary effect of his own experience as a mourning and pardoned sinner is to quicken his sensibility. It is now not the sympathy of the man, but of the Christian, who has learned the source and bitterness of all sorrow as springing from sin. The two conditions of mercy thus meet in his case: sensibility to suffering on the one hand, and the heart to relieve it on the other.

3. *The reception of mercy from God binds upon him the duty of exercising it to others.* It is simple mockery to plead mercy to ourselves, whilst refusing it in our turn. In the parable of 'the unmerciful servant,' (*Matt.* 18:23-25), the

principle of the divine administration is plainly asserted, that our treatment of others shall be the sign of God's treatment of us; and our Lord expressly says, 'with what measure ye mete it shall be measured to you again.' Thus it is, that the spirit of forgiveness is made the evidence that we are ourselves forgiven.

God's mercy branches in two directions, relieving the *woes*, and pardoning the *sins* of men. In like manner our mercy will discover itself in acts of *charity*, and of *forgiveness*. Three principles regulate the dispensation of mercy, under the aspect of *charity*. First, *That we operate in our own sphere as providence may direct.* This restrains from all quixotism in our benevolence, so that we do not break in upon the settled order of society. It renders benevolence more pervading, by making it an individual obligation. Whilst we are not inhibited from associating with others in the management of large public trusts, personal agency of the individual is drawn out in his own sphere; thus correcting the tendency of associated efforts, to do good by proxy. Secondly, *The duty of charity is proportioned to our ability.* If a two-fold conviction could be wrought in the heart of the church, it would revolutionize the world, that our means, great or small, are committed to us as a *trust*; and again, that in all these acts of mercy God simply takes us into fellowship with him, and makes us the almoners of his bounty—so that it is God's mercy *through* our mercy. Thirdly, *The distribution of charity is to be tempered with discretion.* God's mercies are part of an educational process, by which we are trained for glory and immortality. According to the proportion of our wisdom we should have reference always to the real welfare, temporal and spiritual, of the beneficiary.

But mercy in God has its highest manifestation in the *forgiveness of sin*, and so, the forgiveness of injuries is the highest and most difficult exercise of mercy with us. This difficulty is greatly enhanced, also, by prevailing misconceptions as to what forgiveness involves. Two or three distinctions are important.

1. *That we discriminate clearly between the offender and the offence.* The duty of protesting against wrong is often just and obligatory as that of forgiveness itself; and the apprehension of lowering our testimony as to the one, creates no little embarrassment as to the other. The two are clearly separable. God is none the less a God of compassion and love, when he banishes the wicked from his presence.

2. *The duty of forgiveness is absolute, irrespective of the offender's attitude to us.* But say some, God does not forgive without repentance, which makes it a necessary condition of forgiveness on our part. But if this were strictly true, it must be remembered God is not a private person, but a law-giver and a judge, which breaks the analogy. However great the yearnings of his compassion, the integrity of his government and law may require him to punish. This is his prerogative which he challenges for himself, and prohibits our encroachment upon it, (*Rom.* 12:19). In fact, however, the statement is not strictly true in reference to God. His pardon is *free*, through the atonement of Christ, and the repentance itself is his gift—the fruit of the pardon, not its cause. The mistake

consists in confounding the pardon with the manifestation of the pardon to the transgressor's own conscience. In order that the sinner may enjoy the sense of God's free pardon, the gift of repentance is bestowed. In like manner, if we were able to work this grace of repentance in another, we might require it. As it is, our duty is simple and hearty forgiveness, and the remission of all the issues involved to the great and impartial Judge above.

3. *Forgiveness does not necessarily include restoration to full confidence, as before the offence.* In many cases this is simply impossible, because the offence may disclose attributes of character, which, if previously known, would have forestalled confidence and complacency in the first instance. The forgiveness which God bestows is accompanied with a spiritual renovation. We have no power to effect this change; and are never bound to take an unworthy person into our affections. Nay, it may be sometimes our duty to protest against a wrong which we heartily forgive, by the withdrawal of intercourse—not as an act of resentment, but as a judicial testimony against sin.

4. *The Christian seeks, as far as in him lies, to cover all sin by the atonement of Christ*; hoping and praying that, through the sacrifice of Jesus, all sin, in himself and others, may be forgiven at the last day. The effect of this atonement upon himself, and the consciousness of perpetual ill-desert, melt the heart and render him incapable of malice or of wrath.

'*The merciful shall obtain mercy.*' This is their promise, and it is redeemed.

1. *In that, the spirit of forgiveness is the attesting seal of their own pardon from God.* It does not arise from easiness of temper, or from natural placability, much less from insensibility of spirit, or indifference to virtue. It is a divine grace wrought in the soul by the Holy Ghost, and flows from the freeness of God's forgiving love. In this sense, 'they obtain mercy.'

2. *In that, throughout his career, the manifestation of God's mercy is renewed to the Christian.* He daily sins, and is daily forgiven; and there is a daily sealing of God's mercy upon his own conscience and heart.

3. *In that, God's mercy will be ratified, and publicly proclaimed at the last day.* That which was before the secret of Jehovah's covenant, known only to himself, will be published to the universe to his eternal praise and joy.

What a picture this world of sorrow would present, if God's mercy to us were duly reflected in charity and forgiveness to our fellow man! The desert would blossom as the rose, and the widow's heart would sing for joy; and the wickedness of the wicked, like the passion of the serpent, would sting itself to death in the charmed circle which this divine charity would draw around it.

25

The Pure in Heart [7]

THIS phrase is beautifully descriptive of the believer's inwrought and personal holiness; consequently, this beatitude covers the whole process of sanctification from the moment of the new birth to that of the Christian's translation to heaven.

The necessity of personal holiness will appear:

1. *From the operation of the same principles which lead to the reception of Christ as our righteousness.* Undoubtedly, faith in its *principle*, is the gift of God; yet the *act* of faith is our own. The Holy Spirit enables us to believe, but it is we, ourselves, who do believe. Christ and his righteousness are accepted by a free and supreme choice of our own will, as we are persuaded and enabled to exercise that choice by the Holy Ghost. In order to do this, there must be a clear discovery of the beauty of holiness, and of Christ's obedience as exactly commensurate

[7] Appeared in the *Southwestern Presbyterian,* February 17, 1870.

with all the requirements of the divine law. But the same complacency in the holiness of God, which leads to this appreciation and embrace of the Savior, will be manifested in proportional endeavors to reflect this holiness in our own character and life. To suppose the contrary involves a perpetual contradiction, and converts a Christian profession into a solecism.

2. *Personal holiness is the necessary result of the new spiritual life.* The new birth, of course, precedes faith, which is the evidence and fruit of spiritual life, as the breath is the sign and proof of natural life. It is the property of life whenever it exists, to diffuse itself at once through the entire man. We can never say it is here and not there, because it is everywhere, and has its seat alike in every part. Animal life pervades the whole body; it paints the cheek, illuminates the eye, rushes its warm current through the veins, tingles along the nerves, trembles in the voice, informs and actuates the entire frame. Just so, the spiritual life expands through all the faculties of the soul, tinges every thought, kindles every emotion, tones every purpose, and breathes a character into every act. The vigor of the life, in the one case as in the other, may be more or less intense; but, in either case, it is pervasive and entire. Holy living must, therefore, in its various degrees, be the fruit of a spiritual quickening.

3. *Personal holiness results from union with Christ.* This union exists in law, by virtue of which, his work is imputed to us. It exists, also, in fact, by virtue of which His life becomes our own. The union may be mysterious, but it is none the less real. If, then, we are members of

Christ, we must be spiritually conformed to his glorious and blessed image. If he, as our Priest, has 'magnified the law' by his own most perfect obedience, can he, as King, disown that law by canceling or relaxing its claims upon his subjects? This would be to undo, in the application of redemption, all that he accomplished in achieving it, and grace would contradict itself.

4. *Personal holiness is necessary to constitute our meetness for heaven.* This must, of course, depend upon the inward character. Restoration to the divine favor is but a fiction, where there is no capacity to enjoy it. Whilst, therefore, imputed righteousness gives us the title to heaven, our fitness for it is secured through sanctification.

'Purity of heart!' How exactly the word defines the nature of true holiness! Within its critical edge, it cuts through to the heart of all Pharisaism, formalism, ritualism, and merely external morality. There are two tendencies of human thought which it places under arrest: the one, seeking to satisfy the conscience with the decencies of morality, irrespective of the hidden exercises of the soul; the other, taking up with a mere cultus or worship, and satisfied with the simple ceremonies of devotion. This, as DeQuincey has so well shown of the heathen religions, is often frightfully disjoined, even from the practice of the plainest moral virtues. But, as true religion lies immediately between the soul and God, Christ signalizes this 'purity of heart' as its distinguishing feature. Its foundation is laid in the complete rectification of man's fallen nature by the Spirit and grace of God. All holiness is but the development of what is portentially[8] included in regeneration. Hence the gospel is called, with such emphasis, 'the power of God unto salvation', The same original divine power being required in the second, as in the first creation. It further suggests the continued operation of this grace, in controlling and sanctifying all the faculties of the renewed soul. So that what providence is to the first creation, this sanctification is to the second. In both the one and the other, it is not inaptly represented as a continued creation. And finally, it necessitates a due expression of this holiness, in the Christian's walk and conduct. However hidden the springs may be, they are always evinced in the gushing streams; and so long as the sacred flood brews in the secret wombs of the earth, some rift in the mountain rock will send it forth to dance and bubble before the eyes of man.

The promise is made to the pure that '*they shall see God.*' This vision is both present and future—the vision of faith, and the vision of sense. There is even on earth a spiritual discernment of God in the glory of his nature and in the sweetness of his personal relations to us. As these precious disclosures are made to our faith by the Holy Ghost, there is a perfect satisfaction to the soul in the vision. As sight is the inlet of our largest pleasure, it is used in Scripture as the most expressive metaphor for the enjoyment of God. Love feeds upon the sight of its

---

[8] It should not escape the reader's attention that Spirit-wrought regeneration does not make holiness merely 'potential,' but rather is a 'portent' of its certainty. In other words, what Palmer means to communicate is that growth into holiness is a certain supernatural effect of regeneration.—*Editor.*

object, and never tires in its contemplation. So the soul longs for the view of God in Christ, and by faith it sees and is satisfied.

But the perfect vision will be that which is afforded to the saint in glory. Here we 'see as in a glass, darkly;' but there, 'face to face.' Now we know in part, then we shall know even as we are known. Language fails to represent even what thought faintly conceives of this beatific vision. It is enough to say with the seraphic John, 'Beloved, now are we the sons of God; and it doth not yet appear what we shall be—but we know that when he shall appear, we shall be like him; for *we shall see him as he is.*'

26

Blessed Are the Peacemakers[9]

THE seventh beatitude completes the delineation of Christian character, and forms the climax of the series. The justified believer, who, in the fourth, is 'filled with righteousness,' exhibits the power of the new life in the attributes of mercifulness towards men, and of holiness towards God. The grace—which parts in these two directions, enclosing, so to speak, the delta of his sanctification—unites, at last, in this benediction, which covers the whole doctrine of Christian activity and usefulness. It bears, too, a near relation to the preceding 'pureness of heart': for as sin is the source of all schism and strife, it must be dislodged before one can be the maker of peace to others. The fundamental idea here is, that a sanctified Christian is in full sympathy with Christ as the Redeemer of sinners; and ranges himself under his banner of peace, laboring for the reconciliation of a lost world to God.

[9] Appeared in the *Southwestern Presbyterian*, February 24, 1870.

There are two types of piety, both of which are partial and defective, so long as they are exclusive of each other. The one may be defined as the religion of the cloister, where the Christian surrenders himself to the private offices of devotion, and cultivates the graces of the Spirit in solitary communion with God. The other may be designated the religion of the market-place and the forum, where piety takes the form of public service in all the activities in which an aggressive church is called to embark. The due combination of the two gives the highest style of Christian character, in which the believer, supremely jealous for his personal salvation, crowns his profession with a full consecration of all his powers to the Lord's work. Four reasons may be assigned why Christian activity is indispensable in the full development of a true religious experience.

1. *It is God's method, under all the forms of life, thus to develop the latent powers which he has bestowed.* In physical life, for example, the young infant has, at birth, all the sinews and muscles that are necessary for motion; but these lie unstrung and nerveless, until, hardened by exercise, they become the cords of steel which line the brawny arms of the laborer. So with the mind; the intellectual powers exist, at first, as mere capacities, to be drawn forth by culture and use. An imperceptible education begins in the very cradle. The first observation has to be made; and then, the first comparison; and then, the first judgment: until, by sedulous cultivation, the intellectual giants are formed, such as a Milton, or a Locke, a Bacon, or a Newton. Undoubtedly, the same

law holds in grace. The new life, implanted by the Holy Ghost, has its normal development; and all the virtues of a Christian character grow under the operation of this law of exercise. Hence it is, we are put in the midst of duties, in the proper discharge of which every grace is called into action; and there is a clear correspondence between the enjoyments of religion and the daily practice of its virtues. Even the impertinent Charlatanism, which deforms the religious movements of the age in which we live, is, itself, an evidence of this law of the outworking of the true spiritual life in all the activities of Christian labor. For a living philosopher has well said: 'There never was a great working idea in the history of the world, that did not carry its own caricature along with it.' The counterfeit proves the value of the genuine coin.

2. *The church is a kingdom, under Christ, its Head, struggling for ascendancy over an immense and organized opposition.* The young convert is not left to drift alone in an unfriendly world. He is bound up in a society; holding communion with his brethren, in truth and charity; and obeying the laws of a great spiritual empire. From the beginning of time this kingdom has been in the harness of a perpetual warfare with the powers of darkness— Christ and his seed contending, through all the ages, against the serpent and his seed. Of course, the idea of the church, as a kingdom militant upon the earth, can be realized only in so far as every Christian is a soldier, with his appointed place in 'the sacramental host,' and fulfilling his allotted functions.

3. *The Christian is active, because of 'the mercifulness' which has already been described.* God's mercy is conspicuously shown in the salvation of sinners. So the Christian, reflecting this mercy, labors in the same direction for their recovery. A human sympathy for his own race will prompt to large and constant endeavors, on the part of one who has such a personal knowledge of the bitterness of sin, and has felt, so painfully, the pressure of the curse.

4. *This activity has its spring in that holiness which so distinctly appreciates the righteousness of Christ.* How can he fail to enter into the whole plan of redemption, considered as a plan? He longs to see God and the law honored by the farthest possible extension of that righteousness, in which the claims of divine justice are so perfectly sustained. For it must be here distinctly noted that the aggressive movements of the church are determined, not by considerations of general philanthropy, but by love to God and supreme sympathy with his infinite holiness. It is thus a constant force, operating at all times, and under all the forms of Christian experience, to the end that grace may be magnified in the salvation of the largest conceivable number of souls.

The direction of this activity is twofold, as it is individual or combined. Every Christian is anointed as a witness for the truth, in its practical efficacy. For this reason God calls his people from every class, places them in such various relations, sanctifies all earthly affections, that this influence may be universally diffused. And for this reason, too, his discipline is so infinitely diversified, that under every form of trial his grace may be found sufficient. But that this influence may not be weakened by too great diffusion, it is also combined in the organization of his church, through whose agency it concentrates as well as pervades.

The reader should not fail to note the climax in the promise, 'they shall be called the children of God.' In the first place, the original employs not the diminutive word, *tekna*, as in 1 John 3:1, 2, but the strong word, 'sons,' the same which is always applied to our Lord Himself, to designate his relation to the Father. It brings out, therefore, the fact of our adoption, as a thing which is declared and proved by this activity in carrying forward the Savior's redeeming work. We are not infants in grace, but the grown up and adult sons of God; not simply the passive recipients of mercy, but working it out as a potential and operative principle, as the grandeur of its results.

In the second place, there is an emphasis in the expression, 'shall be called.' The glory of the filial relation so approves itself in these works of a blessed co-operation, as to be recognized by all men. The heroic character of this public consecration to God comes to be seen and felt; and the true chivalry of the Christian life, made up of great and lofty deeds, is openly acknowledged.

And, finally, there couches in the promise a pregnant hint of future compensation for all this sacrifice and toil, when the benediction shall be expanded in these words: 'Well done, good and faithful servant; thou hast been faithful over a few things, I will make thee ruler over many things: *enter thou into the joy of thy Lord.*'

Reader! pause and think; what is that *joy of Christ* in which you are to enter?

27

The Supplemental Benediction[10]

THE seven beatitudes are followed by an eighth,
which is clearly supplemental. It is developed from
the seventh, and touches a form of Christian experience
altogether too important to be overlooked. When the
spiritual life puts forth its due energies in the conversion
of the world, it awakens the stoutest opposition, which is
intimated in an expanded form in the benediction which
follows: 'Blessed are they which are persecuted for righteousness' sake—blessed are you, when men shall revile
you, and persecute you, and shall say all manner of evil
against you, falsely, for my sake.'

The same unfriendliness, which led to the rejection
and crucifixion of the Master himself, will be experi-
enced in turn by all who go forth to bear witness in his
name. With characteristic candor, he has given timely
warning of this: 'the servant is not above his lord—if

[10] Appeared in the *Southwestern Presbyterian,* March 3, 1870.

they have persecuted me, they will also persecute you;' and their only comfort is, that in all the dreadful struggle with the powers of darkness, their victory is assured in his own—'be of good cheer, I have overcome the world.' It is therefore no slight undertaking, when the peacemakers start forth in their grand itinerancy over the globe, praying men, in Christ's stead, to be reconciled unto God. Hence the divine teacher, in sketching the outline of Christian character in those beatitudes, and in crowning the whole with this description of Christian activity, cheers his followers with the announcement of a special blessing to those who endure shame and reproach for his sake.

The antagonism between the church and the world was proclaimed in the very first promise which broke upon the guilt and despair of the human race, immediately after the Fall. The enmity between the serpent and the woman is an enmity continued, through all generations, between the seed of both. Culminating in that dreadful conflict between the devil and Christ, the warfare is continued in their respective adherents, until the end of time. Whatever triumphs the church may secure over one generation of sinners who may be brought within her pale, the next is sure to be a generation equally obstinate in the resistance of the truth; and so the grand battle is handed down, from age to age. The only truce, which shall bring to her a measure of repose, is reserved for the millennial glory—to be followed, alas! by the great apostasy and the final consummation. We have never been able to withdraw ourselves from the dark shadow of that prediction. We are overwhelmed with profoundest melancholy, as often as we remember that even the splendors of the church's final conquest are to be obscured by that tremendous declension—and that the history of this lost world is to close amidst the gloom of a final and impious rejection of its Lord and King. The experience of the individual believer is but the type of that of the collective church; as the conflict between sin and holiness, in the breast of the one, ends only at death, so the long conflict on a more extended scale in the history of the other, terminates only when the church shall be caught up to dwell in 'the holy Jerusalem' above.

The forms of opposition which the church encounters from the world will, of course, vary with the prevailing ideas of each succeeding age. It is, however, none the less real; and, all things considered, perhaps equally severe in all. Sometimes it takes the shape of brutal violence, and then we have the era of the martyrs. The faggot and the stake constitute the fiery chariot in which the heroes of the church ascend to take their place 'under the altar.' Then follow times of greater gentleness, when philosophy pleads for universal toleration, and refinement and culture bevel off, a little, the sharp angles of worldly persecution. But the same intense opposition to God and truth signalizes itself in the polished sarcasm and the cold disdain directed against the witnesses for religion. It demands no little grace to withstand the steady pressure of worldly ridicule and scorn, while testifying to the reality of things unseen and eternal.

And the virtue, which would have been braced by a naked conflict of will contending against will, often crumbles beneath the withering influence of a sneer. Let not the faithful witness be faint of heart in this bitter struggle. The promise reads: 'for theirs *is* the kingdom of heaven.' The interpretation will be assisted by the emphasis we have indicated in the verb of possession. The readers can hardly fail to notice how the matter of the promise returns to that which was made in the first benediction. Another proof—by the way—that this beatitude is supplemental: it has no other blessing to convey than what was already pledged in the complete survey of the Christian state, before given. Yet there is a difference, not of substance, but of form, betwixt the gift of heaven, as promised in the two cases. As Lange expresses it: 'in verse 3d we have the kingdom of heaven, with all that it *implies*; here, with all that it *imparts*; there, as objectively set before us—here, as our own personal and actual possession.' To 'the poor in spirit,' just beginning to awake to the wants of the soul, the Savior promises the joys of heaven as their final reward. When these have gone around the circle of Christian experience, and have crowned labor with sufficiency, he says, now yours *is* the kingdom of heaven. All that before was to them the object of desire, of hope, became theirs in an assured fruition, as the reward of their fidelity and service. It cannot be expanded here; but there is a singular and thrilling emphasis placed, in Scripture, upon the sufferings of God's people for righteousness' sake—both as respects the warning they convey to the wicked, and the solace they impart to the good. Take but a single example: where the apostle refers to 'the faith and patience' of the Thessalonian Christians in all their persecutions and tribulations; 'which,' says he, 'is a manifest token of the righteous judgment of God, that ye may be counted worthy of the kingdom of God, for which ye also suffer, seeing it is a righteous thing with God to recompense tribulation to them that trouble you—and to you who are troubled, rest with us,' etc. In Philippians, also, he says: 'in nothing terrified by your adversaries—which is to them an evident token of per-dition—but to you, of salvation, and that of God.' With such an inspired exposition of what our Lord means by the promise, 'yours is the kingdom of heaven,' let no Christian faint in the hour of his trial; and let an unbelieving world know that the promise of the saints' recompense, is the pledge of its overthrow.

PART FOUR

Christian Paradoxes

28

Christian Paradoxes—No. 1[1]

A PARADOX is not, as many suppose, a statement contrary to fact, but only an assertion contrary to appearance. It is often the most precise and energetic form in which a truth can be put; requiring both accuracy of thought and a measured use of language, for its due expression. It is simply bringing together two or more statements, which, though in seeming hostility, have a real but hidden ground of reconciliation. The contradiction in language serves as a note of alarm, which rouses the sluggish mind to note the truth concealed beneath. Hence, it is a form of speech abounding in earnest writings, and occurs with great frequency in the epistles of Paul. Take the following examples: in Galatians, 'I am crucified with Christ; nevertheless, I live—yet not I, but Christ liveth in me.' So in Colossians, 'for ye are dead, and your life is hidden with

---

[1] Appeared in the *Southwestern Presbyterian,* March 31, 1870.

Christ in God.' Again, in Corinthians, 'for when I am weak, then am I strong': while in the sixth chapter of the same epistle, he strings a number of them together: 'as deceivers, and yet true; as unknown, and yet well known; as dying, and behold we live; as sorrowful, yet always rejoicing; as having nothing, and yet possessing all things.'

To the child of God, who has been taught in the school of experience, all this is exceedingly plain; and he carries within him the double sense of all these expressions. But to the men of this world, the mystery is inexplicable, and the whole Christian life is a riddle. Much of our testimony however consists in presenting these very paradoxes to their attention; and the reproach of practical religion is canceled, the moment it is discovered how divine grace combines the most opposite elements in the character of the believer. We propose to submit a few of these strange contradictions to the reader, in several successive papers.

Consider then the profound humility and self-renunciation of the Christian, united with true loftiness of soul and the consciousness of dignity. Experimental religion founds upon a thorough conviction of sin and guilt. The Holy Spirit takes the sinner in the midst of his complacency up into the presence of the pure and holy God, that in the light of the terrible contrast he may see how vile he really is. The law is faithfully applied as the instrument of conviction, to his whole character and life—which, however honorable and discreet in the judgment of men, is seen to lack the formal principle of obedience. It is a terrible disclosure to the soul, when the mask of self-deception is once removed and the real enmity against God is felt to exist. Conscience, which has long lain dormant, and which before undertook to deal with the *principle* of sin, rouses itself to the performance of judicial functions; and the trembling culprit quails before its decision, as though it were the decree of the last day. Then comes this act of faith, as soon as Christ is revealed, in which is necessarily involved the entire renunciation of self-righteousness. 'In me,' cries the sinner in the first hour of his trust, 'in me, that is in my flesh, dwelleth no good thing'; and whilst his heart rejoices in hope, his testimony is, 'by the grace of God, I am what I am.'

It is very difficult now to conceive how all these convictions of personal ill-desert can be indulged, without a corresponding loss of self-respect and a consequent depreciation in character. It is just this which scandalizes the man of the world. When these melancholy confessions are poured into his ear, such as may be heard in any prayer-meeting, and are uttered even more pathetically in the closet, he is tempted to discredit them himself, and to doubt whether they are truly felt by those from whose lips they fall. He could entertain no such opinion of himself, without being overwhelmed with mortification and shame. He reasons that parties, who under such avowals, ought not to be able to lift up their heads any more among men, but to hide in the corners of concealment under the oppressive sense of their own dishonor. Instead of this, he beholds the Christian, after these depositions before God, mingling with others with undaunted front, and exhibiting a loftiness of character and a dignity of carriage, such as he has associated only with the highest consciousness of worth and merit. The whole thing is to him an enigma. For upon his view of the case, such humiliation, if it be really felt, must draw after it the loss of all self-respect; which, in the estimation of the world, is the basis of integrity, and without which the most rapid and complete demoralization is bound to ensue.

This then is the paradox. The noblest specimens of human character are to be found amongst men who profess the deepest sense of personal unworthiness, and boldly avow it in the presence of all creatures. The explanation is twofold:

1. That the standard of judgment is not human opinion, but the law of God, which holds the entire race under the same charge of guilt. The shame therefore and the confusion of face, which overtake the penitent, are felt only in the presence of the great God, against whom this evil has been done. As regards man, no other sentiment is cherished than of regret that all eyes cannot be opened to make the same discovery, and all hearts finally take refuge in the same precious salvation. The sneers and reproaches of the world are not dreaded, simply because nothing is required to extort the same wholesome confessions from every human lip, but the saving power of the Holy Ghost upon the heart, 'convincing of sin, of righteousness and of judgment.' Where all are equally involved in condemnation, none are in a condition to become accusers of the rest.

2. The believer rejoices in a full sense of pardon and acceptance with God, which takes away his dishonor. Just as clear as may be his conviction of sin, just so distinct is his conscious appropriation of an offered righteousness. If in himself he is condemned, in Christ he is justified.

> And lest the shadow of a spot
>   Should on my soul be found,
> He took the robe the Savior wrought
>   And cast it all around.

Surely, whilst singing this stanza to the praise of divine grace, the believer can rejoice in the glory of his righteousness, no less than he mourns over the shame of his sin. It is this consciousness of being clean before God in the obedience of his Son, which the world is unable to estimate—and it is just this experience of pardon through the Redeemer, that arrests the process of deterioration which in the case of the impenitent sinner would undoubtedly occur.

29

Christian Paradoxes—No. 2[2]

A SECOND of these apparent contradictions in the believer's experience is the *union of deep reverence and awe before God, with filial confidence and boldness toward him.*

It is impossible that true views should be entertained of the divine holiness and majesty without producing awe. This is the basis of all acceptable worship, in heaven or upon earth. 'Who shall not fear thee, O Lord, and glorify thy name? for thou, only, art holy.' Like the deep bass, in music, out of which spring all its chords and harmonies, this awe of the soul gives the key-note of all our solemn worship. Hence, when Isaiah saw the Lord in his temple, he cried, 'Woe is me! for I am undone; because I am a man of unclean lips, and I dwell in the midst of a people of unclean lips; for mine eyes have seen the King, the LORD of Hosts.'

How, then, shall the human spirit not shrink and cower beneath this revelation of Jehovah's splendor? Yet,

[2] Appeared in the *Southwestern Presbyterian,* April 7, 1870.

just here, is the paradox: it is in this moment of deepest self-abasement when the publican smites upon his breast, and cries, 'God be merciful to me a sinner!' that he makes the nearest approach to the divine majesty, and feels the truest assurance of his own 'acceptance in the Beloved.' Ah! let the Christian but testify what boldness he has before God, in the hour when he is most prostrate in his humility! There is nothing like it in all the intimacies of earthly friendship. What freedom there is in telling God our most secret sins of thought and desire, which we would not dare to lisp to our dearest love, lest the disclosure of so much impurity and unworthiness should snap asunder the bonds of affection! How frankly we confess to him all that weakness of purpose, and vacillation of feeling which we cloak before the world, in the dread of its utter scorn! With what confidence do we roll upon him those sorrows of a wounded heart, which cannot be exposed to any human eye; or which, in their intensity, recoil from the mockery of earthly sympathy! With what a growing ambition do we pour our petitions before the King, which nothing—short of heaven itself—could ever satisfy! See the boldness with which David takes the covering off from his heart, in the sublime prayer: 'Search me, O God, and know my heart; try me, and know my thoughts.' The veil of reserve, which the instincts of spiritual modesty throw around the more sacred and tender emotions of the soul, in our most confidential human intercourse, drops, of itself, in the presence of him from whom concealment is impossible.

But there we do not stand in that dreadful presence, shivering with the shame of humiliating exposure. This is what the world supposes, when it hears the melancholy confessions which strip the penitent bare of all disguise; and it wonders that he does not slink away from that searching gaze, before which he has uncovered all this dishonor. What is its amazement when this naked penitent looks calmly into the face of God, and says, 'Abba, Father!'

Reader, these simple words afford the solution of the mystery. This God, 'glorious in holiness,' before whom the very seraphim are veiled in heaven, is our Father; we approach him through the Days-man, knowing that our guilt is expiated on the cross, while the Holy Spirit seals upon us the full and gracious sense of our adoption. 'In Jesus Christ we have boldness and access, with confidence, by the faith of him.' 'Seeing that we have a great High Priest, that has passed into the heavens, we come boldly unto the throne of grace, that we may obtain mercy and find grace to help in time of need.' 'Having boldness to enter into the holiest, by the blood of Jesus, by a new and living way, which he hath consecrated for us; we draw near with a true heart, in full assurance of faith.'

The Greek scholar knows the peculiar emphasis of this word, translated 'boldness.' The English reader will catch the exact shade of the thought in the English equivalent, 'free-spokenness.' Wonderful mystery of divine grace! That from that undertone of awe, which subdues and controls the heart, the believer should be able to speak out, before Jehovah, everything that is in him. Yet, why should he not? Has not God, with the antecedent knowledge of it all, still loved him with an everlasting love? Have not these sins been 'cast into the bottom of the sea, that they may be remembered against him no more forever'? Has not the conscience been sprinkled with the blood of sacrifice? Is he not clothed in 'the fine linen, clean and white, which is the righteousness of saints'? 'Who shall lay anything to his charge? it is God that justifieth; who is he that condemneth? It is Christ that died—yea, rather, that is risen again, who is ever at the right hand of God, who also maketh intercession for us.' Nothing is needed but that we should be 'sealed with that Holy Spirit of promise, which is the earnest of our inheritance,' in order to extinguish all sense of fear or shame. With a loving confidence, which has no parallel in any of the associations of life, we lay bare every thought before our Father in heaven. And when words fail to embody our feeling, we just think silently in the hearing of him who is quick to catch even the ticking of the heart.

30

Christian Paradoxes—No. 3[3]

WE enumerate among these paradoxes of Christian experience, a *keen sensibility to the sorrows of life, with perfect equanimity and composure of soul.* This world is a world of grief, and its history a record of sorrow. The young infant commences its career with a cry of distress, premonitory of all it must suffer between the cradle and the grave: and the moans we are accustomed to hear in the chamber of sickness show how hard it is to die. Of the countless myriads who have crossed the stage of life, there is not one upon whom the days of darkness do not come, and whose soul is not pierced, at length, by the sharp point of sorrow.

The only resource of nature in these varied forms of suffering is found in stoicism, which is nothing but the paralysis of the affections. To escape the pangs of grief, the heart is turned to stone; and insensibility to

[3] Appeared in *Southwestern Presbyterian*, April 14, 1870.

suffering is attained only by the loss of all sensibility to the pleasures and joys of life. Like the eastern devotee, who stretches his arm aloft, until it is withered to the socket, the stoic labors to quench all the instincts of natural desire, until he is equally dead to enjoyment and to pain. But with the Christian all this is impossible. He is obliged to think and to feel. Sorrow, too, has, to him, the highest significance, as the divine testimony against sin, and as the discipline by which he is to be more and more delivered from its power. A feeling of indifference to the trials of earth, so far from being a state to be cultivated, would be an attitude of rebellion against God. It would be a bold resistance of the very methods by which grace seeks to subdue more thoroughly his will, and to bring every thought into captivity to the obedience of Christ. The necessary influence of true religion is, therefore, to refine the heart, to quicken the sensibilities, and thus to render more keenly alive to the sorrows of earth.

Just, however, as we are about to rest in this conclusion, and to pour forth our sympathies for a class who seem exposed, defenseless, to the storms of adversity, what is our astonishment in viewing the patience and compassion with which the most overwhelming calamities are actually sustained. Hear the patriarch, Job, exclaim, as eminently the representative of all the afflicted: 'though he slay me, yet will I trust in him.' So, too, the prophet Habakkuk, speaking for all the faithful: 'Although the fig tree shall not blossom, neither shall fruit be in the vine—the labor of the olive shall fail, and the fields shall yield no meat—the flock shall be cut off from the fold, and there shall be no herd in the stalls, yet I will rejoice in the Lord, I will joy in the God of my salvation.' David, also, expresses the sublime trust of the pious, in terms not less emphatic: 'deep calleth unto deep at the noise of thy water-spouts; all thy waves and thy billows are gone over me—yet the Lord will command his loving kindness in the daytime, and in the night his song shall be with me, and my prayer unto the God of my life.'

Human philosophy, in its highest development, aside from the influence of Christianity, could rise no higher than a cold and passive endurance of the ills imposed by a hard and unrelenting fate. But the gospel enables the believer to exclaim, in the hottest earthly furnace: 'We glory in tribulations, also—knowing that tribulation worketh patience—and patience, experience—and experience, hope—and hope maketh not ashamed, because the love of God is shed abroad in our hearts by the Holy Ghost, which is given unto us.'

The explanation of this mystery is, however, very simple. The Christian, in the first place, accepts all from the hands of a gracious and loving Father, to whose will it is a supreme pleasure to submit his own. It is not, as with the ancient Greek, a cruel and impersonal destiny, which grinds, beneath its iron sway, both gods and men alike. But the supreme Jehovah, who asserts his jurisdiction over the whole realm of providence, is a personal friend, who rules in majesty—often in dark and solemn mystery—but who rules with infinite wisdom, goodness and love—having ever a gracious and sweet end in view, the anticipation of which, even by faith, reconciles us to all the methods by which it shall be accomplished.

In the second place, the Christian knows that this is not his rest. The clue to all the problems of life is found in the relation it sustains to the world of joy and of reward hereafter. As in the ocean there is a calm beneath the surface, in its serene depths below, which the rude storms are unable to disturb: so, beneath the waves and billows of human sorrow there is a Christian peace sustained, inviolate, amid all the shocks to which our surface life is exposed.

31

Christian Paradoxes—No. 4[4]

THE apparent contradictions in Christian experience might be extended far beyond what we propose in the present series. The last we shall present is, *the believer's deadness to the world united with the truest enjoyment of it.*

Nothing is more incomprehensible to the impenitent, than this; and no amount of testimony can convince them of its possibility. In the face of a thousand witnesses who certify to the joys of spiritual religion, they persist in regarding it as a life of austerity and gloom. This should not be set down to obstinate incredulity, so much as to the utter inability to conceive of what lies so entirely beyond the range of their own consciousness. 'The natural man receiveth not the things of the Spirit of God, for they are foolishness unto him; neither can he know them, because they are spiritually discerned.' Why even the tears of penitence shed by a Christian over his own

[4] Appeared in the *Southwestern Presbyterian*, April 28, 1870.

sins are sweeter than all the evanescent pleasures of the world. The peace which fills the soul under a sense of freedom, the tenderness of affection toward God when he folds the wanderer again to his bosom, the delight of restored communion with his Father above, are 'springs of joy, unfathomable, divine.' But who knows anything of this, save the man whose heart, melted and subdued by grace, finds a solace even in that unworthiness which draws him so much nearer to the 'God of pathos'? And if the believer finds a happiness even in that which is his grief, how much more should he be able to pluck enjoyment from a world which he treads beneath his heel?

Undoubtedly, everyone who comes into the Savior's kingdom is first brought to the point of a total surrender of this world. Just because it was the idol of his previous worship, this sacrifice is demanded; and whatever may be the extent of actual renunciations afterwards claimed at his hands, he must, in purpose and intention at least, lay it all down at the Savior's feet. 'Whosoever he be of you that forsaketh not all that he hath, he cannot be my disciple.' But how shall that be enjoyed, which has been openly renounced? This is the paradox.

In the *first* place, when the sacrifice has been sincerely made, the sovereign Lord puts it right back into the hands of his children with a free permission to use it wisely, under the seal of his own blessing. The Christian is not called to be an anchorite. It is only required of him, that 'he love not the world nor the things of the world.' The heart is given supremely to God; and when the test of this has been fairly made, a rational enjoyment of life is afforded as his portion here, and as the pledge of infinitely more hereafter. The divine sovereignty is indeed illustrated in the various degrees in which earthly good is bestowed. Some have more, some have less; but, little or much, the Christian receives it directly from the hands of his Father, in covenant loan. The black loaf upon the table of the pious poor is therefore seasoned with grace, which makes it more palatable to his taste than all the sauces of the epicure. This is a grand secret; to receive back from the Lord's hand, as a special gift, what we ourselves placed there in honest sacrifice to his glory—to possess our store, whatever it be, under the cordial sanction of a Father's blessing—and with a clear consciousness that we are enjoying God himself in the same.

In the *second* place, the art of all enjoyment is to be forgetful of it. The essential mistake of most men lies just here: they try too much. Happiness is like our shadow, in more respects than one. It is always and exactly the reflection of what we are, and it follows us with an equal obsequiousness when we walk away from it. Nobody ever caught it by pursuing, and according to the quaint conceit of the Chinese, nobody can succeed in lying underneath it. This is just the folly of unconverted men. The world never can be anything but shadow, to those who mistake it for substance. Even Christians fall into the same error, when the simple enjoyment of religion becomes their supreme end. Just as virtue ceases to be virtue when practiced only for the rewards she brings, so true piety must be sought in and for herself. In every sphere of life, happiness must be the result of what we are—the necessary reflection of those who are careful to stand in the sun. This explains how a Christian can renounce the world and still enjoy it. He knows it to be vanity, and forgets it; and whatever there may be in it of rational enjoyment comes to him with fond solicitation, just because he is wholly independent of it. There is no miracle in the case, nor any reversal of nature's law on his behalf. Rather let us say what sound philosophy itself would teach, that he has found the law of happiness in the oblivion of self. He seeks to be what he should, and to stand accepted with God; and permits his happiness, whether spiritual or material, to take care of itself. He is sure to find that it is as faithful as the Echo.

In the *last* place, this earth is sanctified to the Christian as the sphere of duty. The true significance of life is seen only in its relations to eternity. If a man lives only for wealth, wherein is he better than the ass whose back is galled by the panniers of gold which he bears as a burden? If only for pleasure, wherein is he better than a moth which burns its wings in the candle around which it flutters for an hour? He who lives only for this world, has only at last to lie down and rot. But he who lives for God and duty—who fills up the brief space of fourscore years with deeds of honest service to his fellow-men, and pitches his hopes beyond the horizon of earth, lives to purpose; and the world becomes to him the beautiful temple of his worship. Life, under every other view, is insipid. But it has grandeur of its own, and all its rugged paths are strewn with flowers, when holy acts of self-denial and of toil are daily telegraphed to heaven. It is a luxury to live, when life becomes heroic. The Christian feels ennobled by this consecration to a high and blessed service, which lengthens out through all the eternity that he sighs to enjoy. His pleasure is not to grin and chatter like an ape in the saloons of fashion, where the gibbering nonsense and the soulless laughter bespeak nothing but the empty mind. 'True joy is a serious thing': and it profanes a splendid word to apply it to anything beneath the holy satisfaction of sowing earth with the seeds of noble actions.

The sprouting of an harvest for Eternity,
Bursting through the filth of time.

PART FIVE

*Miscellanies on
Christian Experience*

32

Parleying with Temptation[1]

A MORE striking illustration of the sin and danger
of parleying with temptation cannot be found than
that furnished in the history of Balaam. When the elders
of Moab came to him with the splendid offers of their
king, and with 'the rewards of divination in their hand,'
he was explicitly restrained by the prohibition, 'thou
shalt not go with them.' Yet, when the second deputa-
tion arrives, more imposing than the first, and with richer
bribes, he sets aside the divine will already disclosed to
him; and under the affectation of piety, replies: 'tarry ye
here this night that I may know what the Lord will say
unto me more.' The issue of this sad story is familiar to
every Bible reader. Already seduced from his professed
allegiance to God, he passes on by gradual steps to that

[1] Appeared in the *Southwestern Presbyterian,* December 16, 1869.
Typographical errors have been corrected for ease of reading and
understanding.—*Editor.*

satanic device by which he brought Israel, through open sin, under the judicial displeasure of the Almighty.

In this parleying with temptation, Balaam is but the type of thousands who speculatively receive the truth, and to some extent feel its power; who yet resist its practical control, and by half-deceits suborn the conscience so as to reconcile sin with duty. Taking his case in its suggestive fullness, we may specify four principal ways in which we entertain the tempter and solicit his assaults.

1. *When we reopen for debate an already adjudicated question.* Moralists agree that on all subjects of practical duty, our first judgments are the safest and the best, simply because they spring from an intuitive perception of the right and the true; and that what we call our second thoughts are usually but the special pleading of a dishonest heart to escape from the convictions of conscience. These primary moral judgments, analogous to the instincts of brutes, by their very spontaneity, render to us the truth which may safely be embraced, and the virtue which may rightly be practiced. It is not until these are made the subjects of reflection that they are biased by interest and warped by passion, so as to vacillate in the decision they should deliver. However this may be, in all the temptations of life, the issues should be settled beyond repeal. Only thus can real progress be made in that spiritual education, which the discipline of earth is intended to secure. Human virtue is put to the torture, and one principle after another is settled as the result of the trial. These go into the character of the man, until it is built up in virtue and goodness. But if,

like Balaam, we reopen every issue to a new discussion, how is character ever to be formed? The problems of duty are never solved, a conscience becomes less competent to discriminate between vice and virtue as it becomes more familiar with the aspect of sin; and the tone of authority in pronouncing its verdict becomes weaker, the oftener it is resisted. The sensibility of conscience is its greatest defense. Just as in the human eye, the injurious mote is flooded out in the tears which its irritation produces, so an offence fastens upon a tender conscience till it be removed by healthful repentance and amendment. No greater wrong can be inflicted upon ourselves than to enfeeble the conscience by resistance to its judicial decisions, and to paralyze the will by the vacillation of its purposes.

2. *When we do not strive to subjugate the secret inclination which gives force to the outward inclination.* The apostle gives the genealogy of sin in these remarkable words: 'Every man is tempted when he is drawn away of his own lust and enticed—then when lust hath conceived, it bringeth forth sin, and sin, when it is finished, bringeth forth death.' First then, lust or desire prevails, after which the understanding is gained by the special pleas addressed to it, and finally the will is drawn into the fatal conspiracy, and executes the guilty deed. It is from a state of the heart that temptations derive their power. The thief falls before a solicitation which is absolutely powerless with the honest; and the drunkard succumbs before a proffered indulgence, which does not provoke the appetite of the sober. Of course, the first duty in temptation is

to battle with the secret desire. With this subdued, the strength of the temptation is gone.

3. *We parley with temptation, when we throw ourselves into circumstances of trial counting upon our natural resources.* This is the essential vice in all the systems of reform devised by men, that they build upon the natural strength of the human will and puff it up with conceit. The Bible founds its morality upon thorough conviction of human weakness and guilt, and so teaches to flee from temptation. In this there is a profound philosophy. Sinful man shelters himself under the protection of God's providence and grace; and when thrust out into the fiercer battle with appetite and lust, appeals to the power pledged to him from on high to bear him forward to victory and triumph. His humility is his defense, and his strength is in the sense of his own weakness. The fascination of sin can only be destroyed by turning away from it as from the eye of the basilisk.

4. *The last declension is reached when conscience becomes a conspirator and sin is reconciled with duty.* There is always hope for the most reckless who acknowledge right principles. Something then remains upon which a reform may be grounded. But when the conscience is suborned to render a false testimony, and the very distinction is clouded between right and wrong, man is thoroughly debauched. Hence the value of a Christian education. Even where it does not prove equal to the prevention of sin, it is something to have rendered it uncomfortable. To rob it of all the enjoyments which it promised, is of itself to challenge the transgressor to try the rewards of

virtue. But he who parleys with temptation will find himself, like Balaam, abandoned to his own desire. He will be caught in his own snare, and filled with his own devices. His presumption is punished in the commission of the sin with which he ventured to sport, as victim to the temptation which he has himself invited.

33

Accepted in the Beloved[2]

THERE is an inexpressible sweetness in the language of the Bible. Not only is the truth precious, but the word which utters it is tremulous with emotion. Under the double influence of inspiration by the Holy Ghost, and of the soul's experience of the truth, the sacred writers fell upon a selection of words that come to us dropping with the lovingness of God. How rich in its suggestions, and perfectly melodious, the phrase, 'accepted in the beloved!' *Accepted*: Once separated from God, sentenced, banished, 'aliens from the common-wealth of Israel, and strangers to the covenant of prom-ise;' but now *'accepted.'*

We are too apt to think that we are cut off from God merely through his judicial severity. The necessity of his

² Appeared in the *Southwestern Presbyterian,* December 23, 1869. Typographical errors have been corrected for ease of reading and understanding.—*Editor.*

position compels him to enforce the penalty which law denounces against transgression. This is, indeed, most fearfully true; and no emphasis of language can exaggerate the tremendous fact that the sinner must perish beneath the edge of punitive justice. But there is a wonderfulness in the deeper fact that God's infinite purity separates between himself and the sinner, and that this lies behind all the exactions of justice. It is not the decision of a cold will decreeing judicially the death of the guilty, but our own dreadful departure from the life and holiness of God; this it is which makes us dead in trespasses and sins. As we reflect upon the immaculate purity of the divine Being, the awful chasm widens which separates us from his presence. By the determination of his own unchangeable nature, he cannot look upon sin with allowance—and so the sinner must die beneath his frown.

But divine pity yearned over the lost; divine wisdom contrived the restoration; divine grace executed the reconciliation; and divine love sealed the embrace. The word 'accepted,' covers the whole of this. It reminds us of the estrangement from which mercy sweetly woos us back; of the tender penitence with which we returned again to our Father's arms; and of the generous love which freely forgave, and welcomed us with reconciling kisses. While beyond even all this, the word breathes the fullness of God's own contentment and joy, as he complacently looks into the kindling face of the believer, sweetly reposing upon his bosom.

'Accepted *in the beloved!*' Oh! here is the depth of the sentiment, because here is found the measure of the grace by which we are redeemed and saved. The whole method of the salvation is delicately hinted to the Christian's heart. The grand atonement made for sin stands revealed, by which every legal obstruction was swept away, and by which God can be just, while yet he justifies the ungodly. We are accepted, but only 'in the beloved.' 'There is no condemnation to them which are [in] Christ Jesus.' The problem of justice is solved through the cross; mercy and truth meet together, righteousness and peace kiss each other just there. If these are 'accepted in the beloved,' how perfect the reconciliation! Not, as too often among men, the mere restoration of conventional intercourse, a cold and outward form; on the contrary, we are placed just where the rays of the Father's love fall upon the Son; then through him, upon us. We are in him who is the beloved—and the acceptance which is sure to him is thereby secure to us. Nothing 'shall separate us from the love of God,' simply because it '*is in Christ Jesus our Lord.*' The measure of God's love to the believer is the love he has for Christ. From him it glances upon us—the love of a Father to those to whom he has given power to become his sons. And so it will be throughout eternity. Always seen and always loved only in Christ, the love will be as unchangeable as it is perfect. The acceptance being without reservation, the blessedness will be full, and the joy such as overflows from the Savior's heart into the hearts of his ransomed people forever and forever.

34

I Will Guide Thee with Mine Eye[3]

THIS beautiful expression denotes at once the great-
ness and power of God's guidance of the good; in
vivid contrast with the harsh restraints by which the
stubborn and imprudent are held in check, like the bit
and bridle in the mouths of intractable beasts.

How strange the fascination of the human eye, and
how important the part it plays in all the affairs of life!
There is the look of *direction*, which silently interprets the
will: the look of *approval*, which conveys encouragement
with a tenderness above words: the look of *rebuke*, such
as that of Christ upon Peter, infinitely full of pathos; the
look of *restraint*, which places the heedless or the way-
ward under instant arrest; the look of *love*, which carries
with it a wealth of complacent affection; the look of
contempt, which withers in its disdain; the look of *scorn*,

[3] Appeared in the *Southwestern Presbyterian,* March 24, 1870.
Typographical errors have been corrected for ease of reading and
understanding.—*Editor.*

and the look of *hate*, which sweeps over the heart like the blast of the sirocco, or with the terrors of the hurricane. All this from the human eye: from which, as from a window, the soul looks forth and flashes upon us its varied emotions. This then is the idea: that God establishes with his penitent people such sweet relations, as to govern them with a *look*. The thought is superb. In the grandeur of his infinite nature, God sits upon his throne and sways the whole material universe by the outgoing of a single thought: but in his empire, all his divine affections translate themselves through his eye, and he sweetly guides his own with a look.

Observe, then, *how safely we are directed, amidst the perplexities and temptations of the Christian life, by our quickened sensibilities*. The Holy Spirit dwells in those whom he first renews, and all their moral and spiritual sensibilities are enlivened. It is seldom considered how much our sanctification depends upon the delicacy of the spiritual taste; nor how much we are protected from the evil which is in this world, by the quickness of its perceptions. We have stumbled upon a word which affords the best illustration of the principle involved. The cultivated scholar appreciates, with a relish which seems almost instinctive, all the beauties of a finished style. The connoisseur feels at once the symmetry of a perfect statue, or the combined glories of an exquisite painting. The educated ear is thrilled with ecstasy by the harmonies of music. All these are but examples of what we call taste: which, whether it exists as an original endowment or as an acquired faculty, creates such a distinction amongst men who are of the same race. One looks forth upon nature with 'the dull, leaden eye of an ox:' another drinks in the landscape, until his soul is intoxicated with the beauty. Both have the same organs of vision, and the same faculties of comparison and judgment. But they differ in the power of taste: without which one may have eyes and yet see not. It is not necessary to the pleasures of taste, that we should analyze the emotion. Indeed, like those volatile essences which evaporate in the handling, these delightful emotions of the beautiful and of the sublime escape when we attempt to strain them through the meshes of our logic. It is enough if they spontaneously arise, and we abandon ourselves to a sweet revelry in the pleasure they afford.

Just so it is in the sphere of religion. The conscience and heart are put through a spiritual education, by which the true and the good become things that are *felt*. In the language of one of the best thinkers of our age, 'The very form of the knowledge is love: it is a higher energy than bare speculation—it blends into indissoluble unity, intelligence and emotion; knows by loving, and loves by knowing.' Hence it is that the Bible does not present to us a detailed code of ethics, with the duties of life marked in sharp outlines, as the provinces of a map. It is rather a revelation of grand principles, which are to be taken up, and, with a nice discretion, applied. It fills us with unspeakable sadness to hear professing Christians demand the terms of a literal prohibition, in reference to this or that conformity with the world, when their very education, under the gospel, requires that they should be left to the guidance of spiritual sense in the recognition and application of spiritual principles. A cultivated religious sensibility would at once detect the evil of much that is sanctioned by worldly usage; and the conscience would find its protection, like the human eye, in the exquisite delicacy of its own organization. This appeal to an awakened spiritual taste is clearly implied in the beautiful expression upon which we are now commenting.

It suggests, in addition, that *the Christian's highest joy is found in a present sense of God's love.* The instant he sins, this is withdrawn: when he repents, it is restored. Thus, God's eye, with its look of complacent approval, restrains, directs and guides him through all the intricacies of life. There is much more than a cold recognition of an omniscient surveillance: it is a generous response of the heart, in the full consciousness that all happiness is derived from the beams of his favor resting upon us in the smiles of his love. It is inconceivably precious, that on earth no less than in heaven, God rules us by this law of love: that, here, as well as there, the infinite Father looks upon the children of his grace with an eye whose intelligence directs, and whose love refreshes. Nor can the value of that spiritual education be exaggerated, by which we come to this fineness of feeling and of discernment in religious things, with affections so pure as to be satisfied only with God's presence and approving smile.

Afterword
by Richard D. Phillips

SOME readers might think Benjamin Morgan Palmer an unlikely man to serve as a model for Reformed ministers and scholars in the twenty-first century. Palmer was, after all, a fixture of an era that is sometimes written off as hopelessly 'rationalistic,' and his name is strongly associated with the Southern cause in the War between the States, which many will consider a liability. In fact, Palmer is a shining instance of a servant of Christ who conquered through faith over great hardships and crushing disappointments in life. Those who read his rich contributions to Christian literature will not merely consider Palmer to be relevant to our challenges, but will find in him a great inspiration for optimism and joy in Christian labor.

I could point to a number of reasons for Palmer's usefulness to Christ and the importance of his example. The reader of these *Selected Writings* will have seen ample proof of his remarkable gifts, including a singular gospel eloquence, along with testimonies to his outstanding Christian character. Palmer reminds his readers that *what we do* for Christ always relies and results from *who we are* in Christ. For instance, the tenderness of Palmer's care for the souls who crossed his path is just as inspiring as the wisdom with which he ministered grace to their spirits. In Palmer we see wisdom combined with a loving fervor for Christ's people. Yet above such considerations as these, the reason why I have found myself increasingly drawn to Palmer in recent years is the way in which his high view of Holy Scripture both shaped and empowered his remarkable ministry. Benjamin Morgan Palmer's life and writings demonstrate that strong convictions regarding the inspiration, authority, and sufficiency of Holy Scripture will equip gospel servants with all things necessary to answer the requirements of their times.

The reader of these *Selected Writings* will have noted the way in which Palmer derived both his message and his methods from the Bible. The 'Leaves from a Pastor's Portfolio' provide us with so much more than valued sermon illustrations and uplifting anecdotes from ministry. These vignettes model for us how a thorough grasp of Scripture enables ministers to diagnose and prescribe potently for virtually any spiritual ailment. How could Palmer be so direct and insistent in his counsel to such a variety of problems? Was it a fund of over-confidence on his part or a mere habit of spiritual authority? To the contrary, it is clear from Palmer's sketches that he had become competent in the care of souls through his reliance on scriptural doctrine, precept, and command. As a result, he was able to attend to pastoral matters with a divine authority that directed precious souls to safety. Palmer's example urges that if ministers today desire to be greatly used by God in personal ministry, they should become both competent in the Scriptures and then confident in the authority, truth, and power of the Bible's teaching in guiding their words to the hearts of their people.

Palmer's utter reliance on scriptural truth is also seen in his discussions of church policy. His answers to doubts regarding the validity of church missions provide a model of biblical lucidity. In the face of sociological, psychological, and historical challenges to the spiritual mission of the church, Palmer calmly replies with a biblical mandate. Palmer did not fear the pessimistic attitude of humanism, but rather he feared within the church a 'skepticism as to the truth of God.' 'Yea, let God be true,' Palmer counseled his colleagues, 'and every whisper of distrust and unbelief be silenced forever.' It was by this conviction that he derived his answers to questions of polity and practice in the church, with the result that an outwardly defeated people served Christ's call with so triumphant a spiritual fervor. The missionary endeavors of the Southern Presbyterian churches immediately after a war that had devastated their society erected an imperishable memorial to the power of Christ in the hearts of those who believe his Word. Benjamin Morgan Palmer was instrumental in fostering this gospel vitality through his unshaken conviction in the truth and power of Holy Scripture.

Perhaps most endearing to me, however, is the effect that Palmer's utter reliance on Scripture seems to have had in his personal life. For surely even the casual student of history will realize that these *Selected Writings* from 1869-70 flow from Palmer's pen during a period of a great national convulsion that impacted him grievously. These rich Scripture thoughts on the care of souls, the policy of the church, and the call of Christ to godliness were produced immediately after the crushing defeat of a cause to which Palmer himself was most intimately connected, and in the midst of political upheavals that were certain to bring outward affliction to his people. Yet we observe in this volume the cheerful confidence with which Palmer ministered the gospel in the context of such deep and dark worldly shadows. We know from other sources that Palmer was far from indifferent towards the political cause of the Southern states and church. But one could scarcely know this from these articles and discussions by which he continued to serve Christ and his church. Notice the kingdom focus, with hardly a trace of distraction from worldly calamities. Notice Palmer's undimmed enthusiasm for the least of souls and his undimmed fervor for the advancement of the gospel. Observe the lack of an alloying corruption in his exposition and application of Scripture: no rancor, no distraction, no axes to grind. The evidence of this book suggests that Palmer was simply too consumed by the glory of Christ and his gospel, too firmly committed to the truth and power of Scripture, and too single-mindedly devoted to the spiritual well-being of precious souls that he loved, to be distracted by even the most shocking of outward circumstances or worldly pressures. It is for this reason—Palmer's personal passion for Jesus, his fervent commitment to scriptural truth, and his sacrificial love for people—that he offers such inspiration to those of us who minister the gospel in the chaotic times that we face today.

Having read these stirring *Selected Writings*, let us then reflect on the lessons as they apply to us personally. There are many lessons that will direct us to a sound and biblical policy for our ministry and churches. More significant will be the reflections we make as to *who we are* in Christ, comparing ourselves to this great champion of the gospel, and undertaking the personal spiritual renewal that is needed if *what we do* for Christ will have an impact in our day as what Benjamin Morgan Palmer did had in his.

SOME OTHER BOOKS

from

THE BANNER OF TRUTH TRUST

The Life and Letters of
Benjamin Morgan Palmer

Thomas Cary Johnson

704 pp. | clothbound

ISBN: 978 0 85151 522 9

This biography of Benjamin Morgan Palmer (1818–1902), takes us behind the public figure to the humble, prayerful Christian whose life was marked by affliction. His only son was lost in childhood and four daughters were to die, one after another, followed by his wife. As Palmer saw it, 'The earthly lights are put out that no earthly love may come in between Him and us.'

This is not only a great biography; it is an outstandingly relevant record in an age when the church needs a recovery of spiritual strength and vision. It would be hard to read it sympathetically without being led to pray.

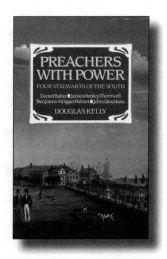

Preachers with Power
Douglas F. Kelly

224 pp. | clothbound
ISBN: 978 0 85151 628 8

Douglas Kelly here reintroduces one of the richest periods of evangelical history, spanning the years 1791–1902, and captures its ethos in the lives of four of its most influential men: Daniel Baker, who spent his life as a missionary and itinerant evangelist though sought by a church and two U.S. Presidents for Washington; James Henley Thornwell, equally able as a pastor and professor but best remembered as a preacher 'wrapt in wonder at the love, humiliation and condescension of the Trinity'; Benjamin M. Palmer, who, in the words of a Jewish rabbi, 'got the heart as well as the ear of New Orleans'; and John L. Girardeau, 'the Spurgeon of America', who was so remarkably used among the black people of South Carolina.

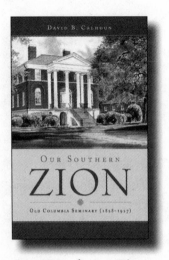

Our Southern Zion
Old Columbia Seminary (1828–1927)

David B. Calhoun

408 pp. | clothbound
ISBN: 978 1 84871 172 3

Columbia Theological Seminary began in 1828 in Lexington, Georgia. In 1830 it moved to the city of Columbia, South Carolina, where it remained for almost a hundred years, until relocating in Decatur, Georgia, in 1927.

Part collective biography and part narrative history, this book follows the story of the seminary during its Columbia years. The title, *Our Southern Zion,* is an expression used by Presbyterians in the Old South for their church and its institutions, including Columbia Seminary.

Southern Presbyterian Leaders 1683–1911

Henry Alexander White

512 pp. | clothbound

ISBN: 978 0 85151 795 7

White's fascinating biographical sketches of leaders in the Southern Presbyterian Church has never been superseded. The better known names read like a roll-call of many of the finest representatives of evangelical piety and experiential Calvinism in America: Samuel Davies, Archibald Alexander, Daniel Baker, William S. Plumer, James Henley Thornwell, John L. Girardeau, Benjamin M. Palmer, Robert L. Dabney, Thomas J. ('Stonewall') Jackson and Thomas E. Peck. But many lesser-known names are also brought before the reader. Here are fervent evangelists, faithful pastors, learned professors, accomplished statesmen, and soldiers—all owing the inspiration of their lives to the saving truths they learned from the Scriptures and the Westminster Standards.

The Banner of Truth Trust originated in 1957 in London. The founders believed that much of the best literature of historic Christianity had been allowed to fall into oblivion and that, under God, its recovery could well lead not only to a strengthening of the church, but to true revival.

Inter-denominational in vision, this publishing work is now international, and our lists include a number of contemporary authors as well as classics from the past. The translation of these books into many languages is encouraged.

A monthly magazine, *The Banner of Truth,* is also published. More information about this and all our publications can be found on our website or supplied by either of the offices below.

THE BANNER OF TRUTH TRUST

3 Murrayfield Road
Edinburgh, EH12 6EL
UK

PO Box 621, Carlisle
Pennsylvania 17013,
USA

www.banneroftruth.co.uk